DON'T BET ON WALL STREET

HOW TO AVOID GAMBLING
WITH YOUR INVESTMENTS

RICHARD H. JENKINS, CPA, CFP®

DON'T BET ON WALL STREET

©2015 Richard H. Jenkins, CPA, CFP®

ISBN-13: 978-1522738435
ISBN-10: 1522738436
Printed in the USA

CONTENTS

DON'T BET ON WALL STREET

Chapter 1 – Don't Bet On Wall Street

"Number one rule of Wall Street, nobody - I don't care if you're Warren Buffet or Jimmy Buffet - nobody knows if the stock is going to go up, down, sideways, or in $%@# circles, least of all stock brokers. It's all a fugazi...it's a fairy dust. "

Matthew McConaughey playing
Mark Hanna in the Wolf of Wall Street

It was October 2007, one of my new clients had just agreed to invest in a moderately aggressive portfolio. I was his financial adviser at Merrill Lynch, and he was tired of watching others ride the market up while he waited around in cash. We had seen a pullback from mid-July until early September, but the markets had returned to July levels and the analysts were saying the worst was over. With the S&P 500 around 1550, he put all of his money into the market. Within a few days, he would be calling me daily to find out how much more he had lost. All I could say was "Hang in there. This is normal volatility." We would later find out that this wasn't normal volatility, but it was going to be the biggest downturn in my lifetime. By March 9, 2009, the S&P 500 would hit an intra-day level of 666. It would take six years for my client's equities to get back to the same level he started. From October 2007 until mid-2015, the S&P 500 grew by less than 4% average annual return. A 10-year treasury bond bought at the same time would have paid 4.5% and would have had a lot less risk.

Wall Street serves a valuable purpose for America. That being said, Wall Street brokers don't always serve that purpose. I was taught that by my father, his father, and most of my family. I came to Wall Street with a healthy dose of skepticism. So, how does one of Wall Street's biggest doubters become CEO of an investment firm? This book tells that story and why I no longer "Bet" my clients' money on stock picking or market timing. To me, "it's all a fugazi." The academic studies show that to be true, but the industry is hooked on selling hope to those willing to take the bet.

Few have had the opportunity to study the inner workings of the big financial companies like I have, even fewer have had the independence and opportunity to act on that knowledge. Before coming to Wall Street, I ran my own family's money. We approached investing as owners of businesses and real estate, the way many wealthy families approach building wealth. Liquid investment accounts were for our next acquisition of real estate, building of a business, and cash flow protection. We never looked at our brokerage accounts as a way to create wealth.

I landed on Wall Street somewhat by accident. It was an outcome of some of the work I needed to do for my family office, not because I chose this path for my career. Intrigued by the volume of money flowing through these institutions, I consulted my way into a position at the largest of the firms on "The Street." It paid the bills, but curiosity was my motivation.

My career on Wall Street was entirely based on finding out how these big firms made so much money in the securities and investment business. I had the same misunderstandings that most investors have, that the good brokers have an edge that makes their clients more money. I came to find out that only a very few have an advantage, and the regulators are constantly trying to eliminate it. The "edge" is actually a structural or behavioral inefficiency that only a few hedge fund managers know how to actually extract from the markets.

This book gives you my view on how to approach your investment decisions with more understanding and on how to avoid betting on markets. I hope I can help a few of you avoid the pitfalls many investors make trusting Wall Street brokers to advise them. The approach I developed is counterintuitive to the way most investment advisers think. I developed the idea from the experience my career provided including accounting, family office, business management, real estate management, investment banking, audit, compliance, finance, strategy, technology, operations, marketing, sales, and investment management.

Working with some very smart hedge fund managers and the top investment research minds in the industry, I found a simple way to extract returns from non-correlated asset classes. This process evolved from the Endowment Method used by the big endowment managers at Universities like Princeton, Harvard, and Yale. The process isn't new and has significantly outperform the average retail investor. It is used by many institutions, but not commonly known or employed by the average retail investor. Until recently, it was difficult to find the investments needed to build this process for accounts with less than $10 million. Even the institutions had difficulty getting the most out of the process until after the financial crisis of 2007-2009. It took a sea change in the industry that came from economic forces that had been building since the early 1970s and reached a tipping point with the financial crisis to make this approach possible and effective for investors.

As you read through this book, you will find out why the process hasn't been used by more Wall Street brokers. The investment industry, particularly in the United States (USA), has profited from telling you that they can help you make more from your investments. As you will read, they know that markets are unpredictable and that stock picking is an ineffectual strategy. Wall Street investment firms profit from selling you research, telling you that they can actively manage portfolios to beat the stock and bond markets, and getting you to buy products that you think "guarantee" your financial future.

What was originally designed to be just a way to match up a seller and a buyer of securities (i.e., brokering a transaction) has morphed into a complex spider web of products and services that use the most sophisticated marketing and sales techniques Madison Avenue advertising agencies can develop, backed by a herd of lobbyists in Washington, and defended by countless legal firms ready to attack anyone suggesting that Wall Street methods are less than fair or honest with their customers. The term "Broker Dealer" used to mean someone that traded your stocks and bonds. Now, it means much more. A "Broker," as it is commonly called, is a firm that is different than an investment adviser. Wanting to have more transactions, brokers made the move to be your investment adviser in order to get all of your investment activity traded through their firms. Years ago, you used to hold your own stock and bond certificates, but now the Broker Dealer holds them in "Street Name." This makes it easier for you to just call your Broker and sell a security with a phone order. In Street Name there is no paperwork, no having to go to the broker's office, just a confirmation that the order was executed.

With the move to being your adviser, the broker became the one that initiated the ideas and handled all of your trades, but he still had to call you. This was called "non-discretionary trading." You still could say yes or no to the recommendation. This generally increased the number of trades a broker did for you, but it didn't go far enough. The broker wanted full discretion to trade your account any way they saw fit, even if the products and services cost more and gave little additional benefit. This lack of objectivity has become cause for concern. Brokers don't have a fiduciary duty and their advice is supposed to be incidental to the relationship. What's even more surprising, the brokers regulate themselves. That's right! FINRA, the regulator for brokers, is a Sell-Regulated Organization (SRO). The wolf is guarding the hen house. I'm not saying that FINRA has done anything wrong, but the rules it enforces come from its own members. Mostly, I have seen proper motivation by member firms and the FINRA board members; however, one has to wonder what happened to objectivity and independence with this regulatory structure.

Unlike Broker Dealers, Registered Investment Advisers (RIAs) are regulated by the SEC, a government agency. RIAs have a fiduciary duty to put their clients' best interest first. What gets confusing is how RIAs have to do business with their clients. An RIA can't hold the securities of their clients. So, the typical RIA has a Broker Dealer hold their clients' securities. The RIA just has trading authority on the investment accounts. This allows the RIA to trade the securities while still letting the Broker report to the client the activity and balances in the investment accounts. For example, you may hire Stone Toro, my firm, to trade your accounts held at Fidelity Brokerage Services LLC.

Sometimes this relationship between the RIA and the Broker gets a little too comfortable. Registered Representatives (i.e., Financial Advisors) of some RIAs can become "dual hatted" by being both a representative of the RIA and for the Broker. These dual hatted representatives can take commissions from the Broker and a revenue share or salary from the RIA. This is commonly known as a "fee-based" relationship with the RIA. Often, it is hard to even know that the representative also received a commission for the products recommended as an investment adviser. When a RIA representative only gets paid for advice, not commissions for product sales, this is called a "fee only" relationship. Several organizations are campaigning to clean up this apparent conflict of interest with Brokers giving advice or RIAs having fee-based relationships. This has become one of the hottest topics for discussion in the industry.

My criticism should not be misunderstood. I admire and have happily worked for many Wall Street firms. These firms have far more people trying to do a good job and help their customers than those who knowingly deceive. I love working with the brightest minds our universities can produce. I admire the innovation and perspective of my colleagues.

Breaking down the walls of these institutions is not the answer. A good sweeping and some honest soul searching probably is in order, but breaking up the institutions doesn't make sense. The economies of scale that make global banking possible, that provide funding for medical and environmental research, that create inexpensive checking accounts and low interest rate mortgages, should be lauded not destroyed. These financial institutions may be in need of some renovation, but not destruction. The financial industry is one of the largest contributors to jobs and GDP, second only to Real Estate in the private sector. Public anger, like seen in Zuccotti Park with Occupy Wall Street, should be acknowledged. Processes need to be changed to better meet the needs of a changing society and a changing economy. Simply breaking up the institutions doesn't address the issues nor change the bad behavior.

Knowledge is the beginning of wisdom. I hope the knowledge I share in this book will help you make wise choices with your financial future. It is my desire that you won't need to have 35+ years of training and experience like me before discovering how to preserve and grow your investments and map your lifetime wealth-building strategy.

If you find this book helpful, I'd like to hear from you. I want to share my knowledge and help investors reach their financial goals. I'm sure more than a few of you will want to challenge this approach, and I'm fine with that. Call, email, or write me and let me know your thoughts. I look forward to hearing from you.

Chapter 2 - Something Changed

"The Chinese economy just overtook the United States economy to become the largest in the world...when you measure national economic output in "real" terms of goods and services."

BRETT ARENDS, MarketWatch, Dec 4, 2014

"China overtakes US to be biggest economy [measured using GDP] by 2024."

SZU PING CHAN, The Telegraph, Sep 7, 2014

What happened to the good old days? The days when the market always went up and all you had to do is look at fundamental research to pick the stocks you wanted. In 1974, it all changed. Median wages dropped for the first time since the end of WWII. For the average middle-class American family, it takes two incomes and a part-time job to feel as wealthy in 2015 as it did in 1974 on one middle-class income. The number of people in poverty dropped to the lowest level in 1973 and has not seen that level since. 1974 became the turning point for the American economy. Like an engine running out of gas, the surges and stalls in the market since that point just reflect the constant battle companies wage to try and survive this downward trend.

It was May 1981. Between collecting rents, painting apartments, fixing plumbing leaks, and helping keep the books for my family's real estate holdings, I would squeeze in a few hours of study for the CPA exam. I had worked 30-40 hours a week and gone to night school at a state college to get my accounting degree. Jobs were hard to find, and I had taken two extra quarters in college to switch majors just to have a chance of getting a good job. My goal was to work for a "Big 8" accounting firm. I had interviewed with all eight firms. Offers were starting to come in, but I wanted to be a part of the tech boom in what would become known as the Silicon Valley. All eight of the firms gave me offers in their Los Angeles offices. Finally, the Price Waterhouse office in San Jose made me an offer to work in their audit department. If was the highest offer so far at $17,000 per year. What a relief. I could now afford to buy the house we wanted, a newer home for $100,000 in an up-and-coming neighborhood.

Contrast my experience with the college graduates of today. The colleges encourage minimal work time while in school, and frankly, the study, internship, and volunteer expectations are so high that most college students just do not have the time to take a job. This results in a mountain of debt and an eventual realization that a graduate degree is the only solution to get a good-paying job. This comes with even more debt and absence from the job market before incomes can start to pay for the 6+ years of schooling.

I experienced a much different outcome than these graduates. My parents and I had enjoyed the opportunity to get educated, work hard, and better their lives. The post WWII economy had given two generations a chance to do better than their parents. By 1980, the situation had changed. Graduates began to have trouble finding jobs. College was no longer a guarantee of success or a better life than your parents. Some graduates, like me, were able to find good-paying jobs and continue the hope of a middleclass lifestyle. By the time my children starting thinking about college in the year 2000, the situation had changed immensely. In fact, real hourly wages have declined for the bottom 70 percent of the college-educated workforce since 2000 (Lawrence Mishel, Economic Policy Institute, October 3, 2012).

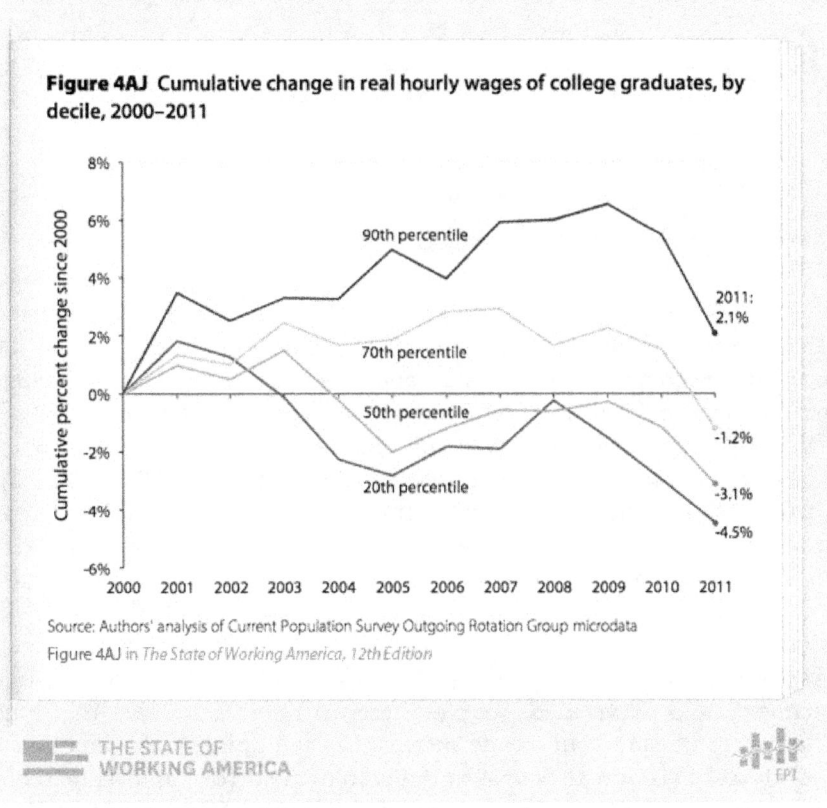

Figure 4AJ Cumulative change in real hourly wages of college graduates, by decile, 2000–2011

Source: Authors' analysis of Current Population Survey Outgoing Rotation Group microdata
Figure 4AJ in *The State of Working America, 12th Edition*

THE STATE OF
WORKING AMERICA

In 1947, U.S. soldiers returned to a country that was the only manufacturing powerhouse left in the world. You could make almost anything, and somebody would buy it. All the other countries had lost their factories to bombing raids and their workers to war-time casualties. By 1974, the developed world had caught up with the U.S. and were ready to compete. The post-war economic boom was over. As Harold Meyerson observes (The Forty-Year Slump, American Prospect, Nov 2013), having run a trade deficit in 1971 for the first time since the 1800s, the U.S. started to lose its upper hand on the world, and by 1976, the U.S. lost the trade war and has had a trade deficit every year since. A broader measure of our trade deficit is the current account deficit. This looks at money moving between nations. It tells the same story as the trade deficit - things changed in the mid-1970s.

UNITED STATES CURRENT ACCOUNT

Current Account (USD Million)

SOURCE: WWW.TRADINGECONOMICS.COM | U.S. BUREAU OF ECONOMIC ANALYSIS

Something other than good management affected companies. Things out of the control of even the best executives. The only solution left was for U.S. companies to globalize and ride the growth of other nations as part of their business strategy. The global economy had begun.

A response to this growing economic pressure was the two-worker household. Traditional gender roles of the 1950's and 1960's had been pushed aside by the women's liberation movement. Men coming of age in this era were accustomed to seeing their mothers and sisters working. As they got married, they expected that the marital roles support the career aspirations of their wives. Also, nontraditional family units (later known as alternative lifestyles) started to emerge. Gay and lesbian couples found communities accepting of their progressive thinking. The role of religion changed, and unmarried couples became more accepted. With these changes came slow, but steady increases in the number of women in the workforce. This added people to the employment rolls and increased the percentage of people in America who were working. Measured by the Labor Participation Rate, this trend continued from 1977 until the year 2000.

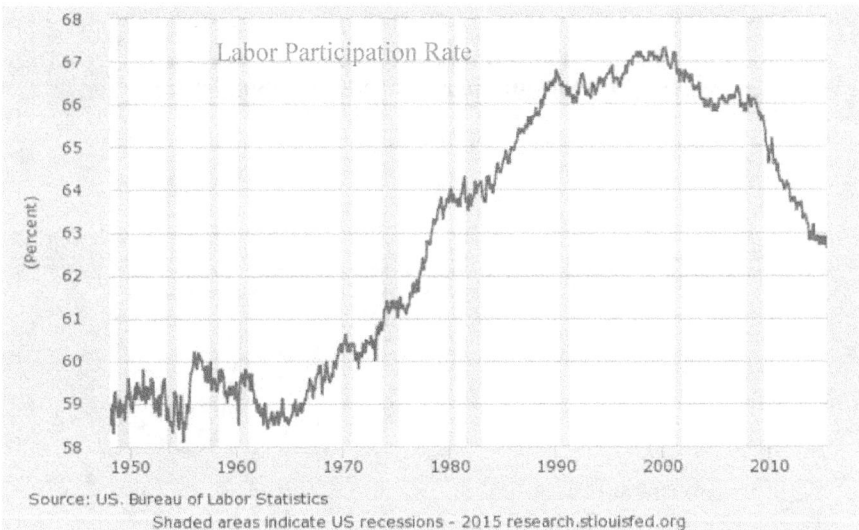

Source: US. Bureau of Labor Statistics
Shaded areas indicate US recessions - 2015 research.stlouisfed.org

As David A. Graham reports in the Atlantic on July 2, 2015 (the above chart from the US. Bureau of Labor Statistics was included in the article), many factors led to the ending of this labor participation in 2000. Baby Boomers started to retire early; some experienced under-employment and unemployment from the tech bubble bursting; and still others were just too disappointed and fed up with the "Yuppie" lifestyle to put quantity before quality any longer. The increase in the number of people not working to those working has expanded since 2000.

U.S. Households defended lifestyle goals against the global economy through expanded work-hours per household. More and more women went to work. People worked later in life. Kids found themselves working through college and taking second jobs to pay for college debt. These efforts to preserve the American Dream required jobs and opportunity, something that changed in 2000.

Mark J. Perry of the American Enterprise Institute notes in his December 4, 2014 research, hours per house hold have been declining since 1999. The following chart aligns with the message of the labor participation rate:

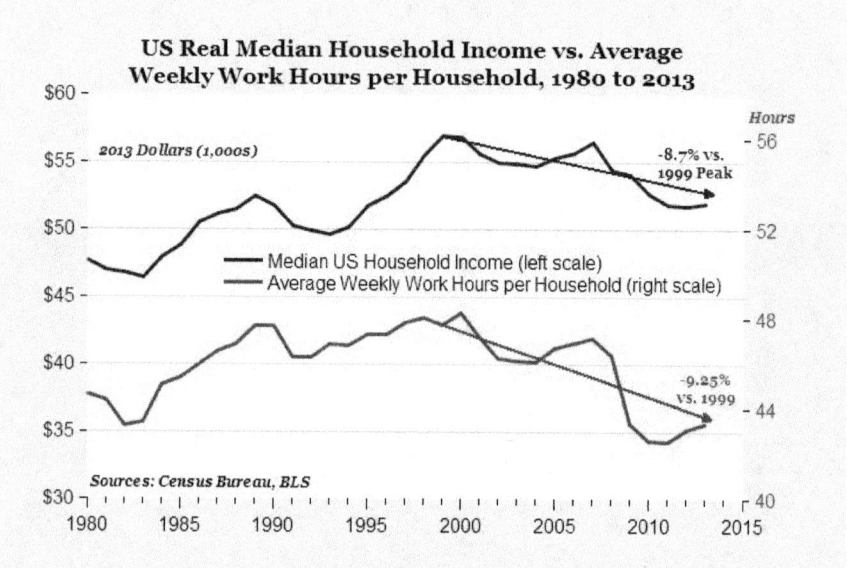

US Real Median Household Income vs. Average
Weekly Work Hours per Household, 1980 to 2013

This inflection point in the Year 2000 continues to show up in the way companies have responded to this shrinking labor population. Some contend that the reasons for this decline includes automation of labor. As more and more jobs get automated away, the required labor pool becomes smaller. Is it companies replacing jobs with technology, or is it technology filling the space of a declining participation of the workforce? Capitalism focuses on building profit. If machines perform the same duties for less cost, then companies in a capitalistic society will tend to choose machines. Even the accounting we use reflects this thinking. Machines are assets and labor is an expense. Certainly, automation does displace some workers, but this is not always a one-way street of companies displacing workers. For example, California companies were forced to develop technology to pick strawberry crops due to labor shortages.

The public assistance and health care needs of this growing population of unemployed are supported by fewer and fewer percentage of people working. As a result, public debt has mounted to an all-time high. Former Fed Chairman Paul Volker warns that debt of federal, state, and local governments makes them ill prepared to weather the next recession. As he looks at the situation, Chairman Volker continues by saying, "And I think the probability of a crisis increases as time goes on."

The Trustees of the Social Security System appear to see the same crisis coming. In their report of May 2013, they projected the funds to support the system would be exhausted by 2033. The Congressional Budget Office (CBO) has similar dark projections with budget deficits expected to rise in the coming years forcing up debt levels well above 100% of GDP. This would be like having more debt than your annual income, not uncommon if you include your mortgage, but fairly high nonetheless. The history of this debt/GDP relationship matches well with the globalization and labor participation stories.

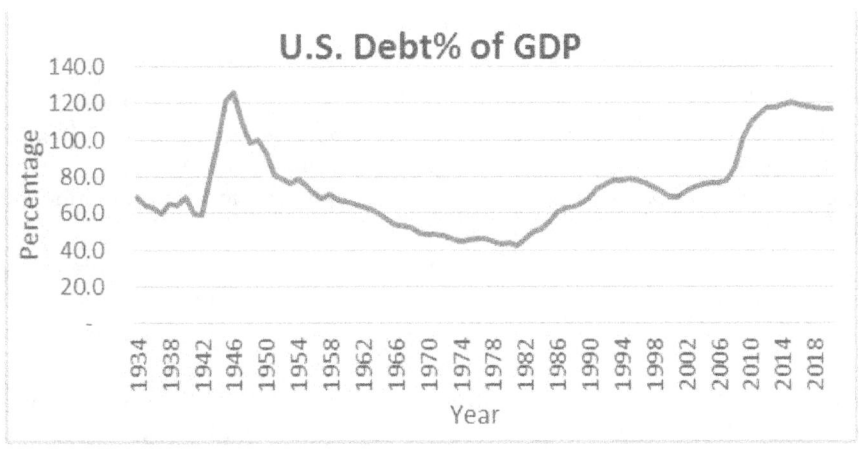

Taxes were about 17.5% of GDP in 2014. This is expected to rise over the coming years. The history of taxes compared to our GDP has varied based on a number of factors. The following chart shows this history:

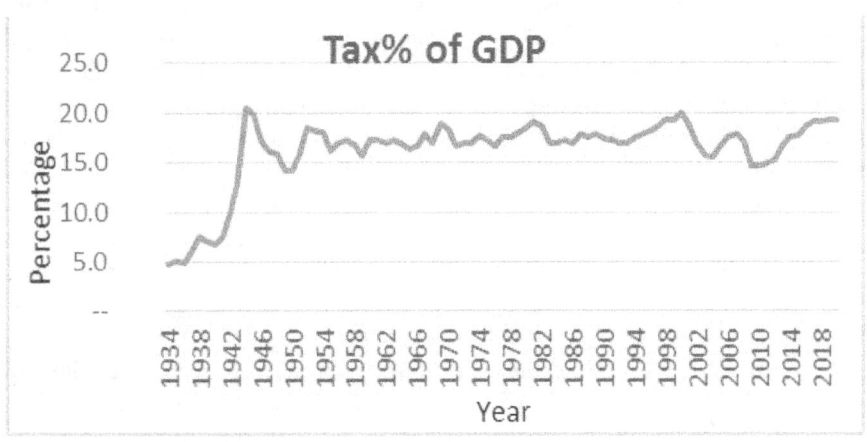

As part of the Economic Recovery Act of 2002, taxes were cut to stimulate growth. This can be seen as taxes as a percentage of GDP drop to levels not seen since the 1950s. The price paid was an expanding debt to GDP level that slid us back to Cold War (1980's) and World War (early 1940's) levels. By 2008, the financial crisis was in full swing, and spending by the US government was seen as the only way to prevent economic collapse. This time, taxes had to go up or debt could spin out of control. Even with higher Tax to GDP levels, debt continued to rise since 2008 at the fastest rate since World War II. While debt to GDP levels are expected to moderate in the short run, the CBO projects significant increases in this rate exceeding 200% by the end of the 21st Century unless something is done to prevent this.

Reflecting on this information, it is clear, something changed in the early 1970's that put in motion many social and economic responses still being felt today. The next inflection point was in 2000 with the tech bubble bursting. The aging population, lower household labor and earnings, and the economic impacts of debt and taxes are taking a toll on the American worker and the companies in which they work.

The investment community has been impacted by this as well. In Chairman Volker's words, "markets can change dramatically, and it's almost instantaneous and with no notice." The use of history as a tool to predict investment markets seems to be less and less effective. Just when you think you have an investment strategy that works, the "instantaneous" change wipes out years of investment gains. Called a "tail risk" by investment professionals, the only response that seems to give solace during these events is "hang in there and it will come back." Not very comforting to those who have lost 65% of their wealth to a market crash.

Another interesting thing happened in 1973. Burton Malkiel of Princeton University published his research in a book called "A Random Walk Down Wall Street." He contended that active investment management, including stock picking and marketing timing, were ineffective at outperforming the market. Since markets tended to go up, just buy the market and invest for the long run, he recommended. This made the most mathematical sense given the data of the post-war economy that Malkiel used in 1973. Markets had always gone up, at least in any meaningful period of time. If you can't beat them, join them was his approach. By 1975, John Bogle had the same idea and started Vanguard to give investors a low-cost way of buying the "market." Is this still a good approach? Let's examine this idea.

In the 15 years from the market peak in March 2000 through the end of March 2015, the buying power in the S&P 500 barely broke even. While there was a real dollar rise in this broad-market index, the impact of inflation and taxes on buying power significantly impacted the investor's experience. The buy and hold strategy is failing to provide what it promised. Despite all the risk an investor took to get a better return, the 15-year result was no significant increase in the inflation-adjusted U.S. stock market. The old paradigm "more risk, more return" actually didn't work over this peak-to-peak period. For the ten years of 2004-2013, the average blended equity and fixed income retail investor only earned 2.6% per year against an inflation number of 2.4% for the same period (Forbes, April 24, 2014). Had this average investor only had stocks and no fixed income, the outcome would have been much worse. Even so, the risk of both the stock and bond markets during this period were greater than any previous 10-year period with the reward being effectively no real return on investment.

Retirees suffer even more with this reality. If you retired in early 2000 at the age of 65, this reality means that you probably are running out of money. Your cost of living rose even faster because of out-of-control health-care costs and other costs of aging. With the good news of living longer, middle-class savers who retired in 2000 have to face the reality that they are likely to run out of savings. Many already have. As a result, a much higher percentage of our aging population will need help with their living costs than ever before. What impact will this have on companies? Higher taxes perhaps to support our elderly poor?

The one bright light in this dim truth of our economy has been the bull market for bonds. Rates have been steadily decreasing since 1981 from a peak 10-year treasury rate of about 15% to a low of about 1.5%. This added bond appreciation to the coupon rates. If you bought a bond at say 12% and rates went to 10%, your bond value went up provided there was at least a few years left before the bond matured. You get both the 12% coupon and the appreciation of the bond value. To realize this capital gain, you needed to sell the bond. That was fine if you wanted to spend the money; however, if you wanted to reinvest, you would just buy another bond with a longer maturity and do the same thing all over again when your 10% bond went to 8%. The bond management business exploded promising to extract this bond appreciation from your portfolios. Now, in 2015, the bond manager finds it hard to justify a 0.5% management fee for a 1-3% coupon and no bond appreciation. Will rates go back up? This is the ever present risk that long-term bond investors face worrying that they may not even keep up with inflation if rates rise in the future.

Even the counterbalancing effects that bonds used to provide a diversified portfolio have been fading. By the end of 2014, bonds were moving in concert with stocks 60% of the time. The risk-dampening effects of having both bonds and stocks in a portfolio have become undependable. Bonds become even more correlated with stocks in economic downturns. The risk-reducing qualities of bonds are happening less and less frequently, especially during times you need the non-correlation most, during stock-market crashes. "Buy bonds for safety" has become increasingly hard to justify. If the central bank rates go up or if inflation rates go up, the likely outcome is for bond rates to rise. This typically results in a downward price movement in the bond value. It has been a long bull run for bonds, but the investment bet on bonds is getting harder and harder to make.

Several smart investors have proposed using international markets to build long-term value. In a Dec. 30, 2014 Wall Street Journal article, Burton Malkiel proposed that the less risky play was the international markets. U.S. markets were significantly more expensive than international markets, and this would self-correct in time, he predicted. What if the correction is for U.S. markets to decline, not international markets to climb? The bet is on the difference between the markets, not on the international market doing well. That is to say, his observation of this dislocation between market valuations historically corrects by capital flowing to the cheaper market. Sometimes the capital within an investment economy creates the self-correction. For example, U.S. capital may flow out of U.S. stocks to cash or debt reduction instead of flowing to international markets. If this happens, the flow out of U.S. stocks will likely decrease the U.S. stock market levels, but not improve the international stock markets. On a relative basis, the investment in international stocks over U.S. stocks may make sense, but both markets may still go down. The concept of "migrating risk" sounds reasonable, but it still relies on calling markets, something Malkiel himself contends you just can't do. When there is nothing else available, this risk migration strategy may be the best technique available, but it still has a hard time creating outperformance. This has been demonstrated by studies that examine the impact of active allocation (e.g., Gary Brinson's "Determinants of Portfolio Performance II: An Update").

Instead of buying the U.S. market, perhaps the new approach should be "buy the global market for the long term." With Greece and China's economic issues, global political unrest, and a list of many other market-rattling events, the old expression that "When America sneezes, the world catches cold" may just become a reality. No one can predict the outcome of any economy or market. Betting on one over the other is just that, a bet. If we truly are in a global economy and companies have generally adapted to this, one might assert that the best one can do is buy the global market. This would be the logical extension of the work Malkiel did in 1973 when the U.S. was the dominant economy.

Today, there are many economies that are growing faster than the U.S. Companies benefiting from those growth rates should outperform the U.S. overtime; however, trying to pick which stocks and which countries is likely to be just as difficult in a global economy as it was in the studies that Malkiel and Brinson did on the U.S. markets. But what if the global economy starts to show the same downward trend that the U.S. has shown since its peak in March of 2000?

When we look at the global equity markets not including the U.S., we find that the story is even worse than the U.S. stock market. From March of 2000 peak, the U.S. stock market has outperformed the rest of the world by about 70% (MSCI ACWI x-US vs. SPTR Index). There have been times the U.S. markets have underperformed the rest of the world, but out of the financial crisis, the U.S. markets have fared much better.

Predicting the future of any country or region has become increasingly difficult. The trends can reverse, literally overnight. For example, consider Iceland. This small country was fast becoming a banking destination for the world when its economic power was wiped out overnight due to just three banks that had debt of more than 11 times the national GDP.

I can appreciate the frustration that great investment minds have in accepting that published studies effectively tell investors that the only value investment managers provide is in aligning and maintaining an acceptable level of risk in the portfolio. The one thing the investor wanted – to predict the market – really could not be done. This frustration led to using these studies to support ideas not intended by their authors.

Asset allocation is one such idea. The industry locked onto the asset allocation concept, but with the message to the investor that this was how they would improve returns. For a time, the ever-present search for returns by investors was satisfied by the assertion that asset allocation, over time, would outperform market timing and stock picking. Of course the most important part of this assertion is the "over time" factor. This meant that investors would not be able to judge their investment advisers until several years in the future. As long as stocks and bonds acted differently and cash kept up with inflation, the investment managers were able to point to the smoothing effects of asset allocation. So, from around 1991, this became the message to the investing public, and it worked. It wasn't until the 2007-2009 downturn that investors began to question this message. When everything in their portfolios failed under the weight of the global financial crisis, including money markets and bonds, they began to doubt the message that asset allocation was the answer.

This is a good point to stop and reflect on these changes. The U.S. started to lose against other economies starting in the early 1970's. Studies in the 1970s, 1980s, and 1990s showed that stock picking and market timing really didn't help much. While asset allocation improved return to risk ratios, active asset allocation didn't add much, if anything, to portfolio returns. The best an investor could do before 2000 was to buy a well-diversified portfolio for the long term. Then, we entered a new era. The U.S. stock market failed to have an increase in real buying power from March 2000 to March 2015. Asset allocation seemed to not provide effective investment protection in the 2007-2009 downturn. Wages and labor participation started to suffer. Something truly had changed.

Chapter 3 – React, Don't Predict

"A man should look for what is, and not for what he thinks should be."

Albert Einstein

Until now, investment professionals have focused on finding a way to predict if an investment will go up or down. The studies showed that their effectiveness on predicting was no better, and often worse, than the average market returns. Some investors tried to find an "edge" to give an advantage to their predictive powers. Many of these techniques have now been regulated away to make for a fair playing field. The focus for years has been on building better math models and faster reacting machines to take advantage of the unaware or slow-acting investors. These approaches tend to lead to the machines acting unpredictably and loosing large amounts of investor capital. Once asked if the market would go up or down, I respond "yes." While meant to be humorous, it reflects a simple reality – that markets will go up and down. Wouldn't it be nice if there was a way to let the markets do what they do and profit from the up and down movement? Using this simple idea is what I discovered seems to be helping the smart money do better than the rest of the investment strategies.

The Wall Street Journal ran an article on July 24, 2015 titled, "Advisers' Stock Recommendations Drag Down Clients' Portfolios, Study Finds." The author, Daisy Maxey, points to the working paper of Meir Statman, a professor of behavioral finance at Santa Clara University in California. Professor Statman is quoted as saying, "when they [advisers] try to beat the market by trading, they are more likely to harm clients than help them." This is consistent with the work of Dr. Malkiel at Princeton and reflects a truth that makes investors question the value of investment advice. Up until now, what has been the adviser's value? To answer this, other research studies have been conducted. In the same WSJ article noted above, another study is cited that shows that "advisers help investors to be more diversified and avoid common pitfalls." Is diversification and pitfall avoidance what investors thought they were buying for their money? Most investors I know ask advisers to "help me make a better return on my investment." Granted, risk avoidance may be a genuine benefit, but return is the goal for many who hire an adviser.

Many advisers have adopted the approach of educating investors that risk management is more important than great returns. They used this approach primarily because they didn't have a solution for better returns. One bad step in the investment world could be very costly. This is true, but that doesn't mean you should accept the current investment environment of stocks and bonds as the only way to achieve a reasonable return on your investments. Risk management in combination with finding investment solutions beyond stocks and bonds needs to occur to solve the investment return issues.

In the past, risk was reduced by adding more cash or bonds to a portfolio. Cash would keep up with inflation, and bonds traditionally meant a lower return than stocks. The prudent, risk-averse investor allocated more to bonds while the risk-takers went for more stocks. This was the world our parents and grandparents knew. Life was binary. Up was good and down was bad. You sold if something started to go down and you bought more of the thing that went up. This thinking came from the belief that stocks go up because these are good companies that are succeeding, and stocks go down because something is wrong with that company.

In today's world, looking at things as just binary creates confusion. Good companies sometimes are punished for missing quarterly expectations, even if there is long-term justification for the lower earnings. Bad companies that sacrifice longevity for short-term growth can be rewarded. What is good and what is bad becomes hard to identify. Bonds are no exception. When rates were stable or declining, bonds were easier to price. Now with liquidity premiums, credit spreads, and monetary policy constantly changing, bond prices become much harder to understand.

Recognizing that advisers have not been successful in calling markets and picking stocks is the first step towards finding a solution. Recognizing the problem establishes the opportunity to find a better way. I established my research to solve this very problem. My core question, "Is there a better way to invest, today?"

To answer this question, I drew upon some wisdom that had produced my family's wealth. In the early 1970's, my father, a physician, asked one of his wealthy patients, "What should I invest in?" Rather than give a direct answer, the wise old patient said, "Whatever the wealthy are investing in!" Observing that all of his wealthy patients were buying real estate, my father began a 20-year program of buying more and more apartment buildings. It worked out very well for him.

I asked a very similar question, "Who has the best performance?" To be more specific, I asked, "Who are the best performing institutional investors through both up and down markets?" I wanted to find the investable strategies that were successful despite the changes in our world since 2000. With this knowledge, my hope was to build an investment approach to help my clients have better results.

In my search for better performance, the usual suspects appeared like Warren Buffett, Ken Fisher, Benjamin Graham, John Templeton, Jim Rogers & George Soros, and Jim Simons. Certainly, there were many "Guru" investor success stories from which to choose. The first step was to separate out the investable strategies from the ones that only the Guru could do. This eliminated Jim Simons, immediately. His black-box technology was highly guarded, and his Renaissance Fund was closed with no similar strategy apparently available to the ordinary retail investor.

Warren Buffett, while highly followed by retail investors, mostly relied on opportunity and size that only Berkshire Hathaway, his company, seemed to have. While the foundation of his strategy is to "buy a wonderful company," it is hard to buy the "wonderful company" he can buy. Big opportunities, like bailing out Goldman Sachs in the financial crisis, were only available to big investors like Warren Buffett. Perhaps, one could buy Berkshire Hathaway stock and let that be the solution. Not a bad history of performance in the stock. The price rose at an average annual rate of just over 9.6% from March 31, 2000 to March 31, 2015 compared to the S&P 500 increase of just under 2.2%. While many investors choose this as their path, I did not want to put my clients into just one stock as their investment solution. Too often, the single manager solution proves to be a bad choice, and even Warren Buffett has had periods of underperformance (e.g., first three quarters of 2015).

Without naming names, several of the Gurus of investing actually were just using the wrong index to show outperformance. For example, one was a small-cap stock investor when small cap was doing well, but he compared his performance to the S&P 500, a large-cap index. As small cap underperformed, he migrated to more large-cap stocks, which brought his performance more in line with the S&P 500 performance. These revelations proved out Malkiel's studies about stock picking not being an advantage over the market. In the investment industry, this process of using a segment of the market to outperform is called a "factor bet." Sometimes this works well for investors. Factor bet outperformance is often followed by unforeseen underperformance, making it very hard to sustain outperformance over longer periods of time with factor bets.

After eliminating the strategies that were not investable and the factor bets, very few strategies showed real promise. The one that stood out for me was the Endowment Method, a strategy made most famous by Yale University. This approach divides up the portfolio by when you need the funds. For current and near-term cash needs, the investments are more liquid and less volatile (i.e., less risky). For core components that may not be needed for a long time, if ever, investments that pay higher returns and have less liquidity are selected. The approach uses an investment policy to identify the approved allocation percentages and relies more on alternative investments. The need to support the goals of the endowment, primarily the operating expenses of the universities, drives the decision process.

Remembering that Gary Brinson's studies showed that asset class was the biggest reason that performance varied from investor to investor, I wanted to know if successful users of the Endowment Method used a particular asset class to achieve their success. In fact, there was a significant difference. They had about 50% of their portfolio in alternative investments. During the 10-year period from June 2004 to June 2014, Yale and Columbia posted an 11% average annual return compared to the S&P 500 returning less than 8% and average retail investors at 2.6%. Private Equity returns were nearly 16% annually during this same time. With so much allocated to higher performing assets, the returns were much higher. But I was not convinced that this was the only reason. The math did not seem to work to explain the entire variation. I was missing an explanation for about 2-4% of the outperformance.

Many theories circulated about the reasons for outperformance by those using the Endowment Method, but no one theory seemed to explain the totality of the outperformance. Some have actually suggested that it is the genius (knowledge, capability, and intuitive powers) that sits on the investment committees that make up the difference. That theory would suggest that a smart enough manager could accurately predict the future of the investment markets; however, we know that the academic studies do not support this theory.

To find the reason for the additional performance, I used my industry knowledge of hedge funds to observe a curious change in behavior by the users of the endowment method. Hedge fund managers had refused to return their investors' money until after the financial crisis. This became known as "gating." This made it difficult to get the cash needed for operations when the investor needed it most. I knew how the endowments and other institutions had solved this problem because I had presented our hedged funds to nearly 600 institutions, many using the endowment method.

As we presented our hedge funds to these institutions, the first question they would ask, "Do you have separate accounts?" At first, I thought they were just avoiding another incident of having their money held back. With a separate account, endowment managers could keep control over when to liquidate the investments, thus, eliminating the gating. What I discovered was something completely surprising. Not only would a separate account help with the alignment of cash flow, but it also made it possible to rebalance the allocations the endowment managers made to these "illiquid" investments. It was this "new" ability to rebalance their hedge fund allocations that made me wonder if something in this process might be giving the added return.

At this point, it is important to note that 1) I am not a part of the Princeton University staff, 2) have no contact with their investment team, and 3) receive no endorsement from them. My only contact with them is as a member of the Princeton Community. I have lived and worked in Princeton for many years.

One of the advantages I had was the ability to tap into the intellects of smart young graduate students from Princeton University. Each year my portfolio managers would hire interns from Princeton. These student interns would bring with them the latest ideas from professors like Burton Malkiel and John Nash. When we had an investment question that needed to be analyzed, you couldn't find a better source than these interns. They would do quantitative analysis for us. They evaluated large amounts of investment data to find the "reasons" behind the numbers. Combined with the experience our staff brought to the table, the research was limited only by our imaginations.

Using this information, we identified that the presence of non-correlation in a systematically rebalanced portfolio helped improve returns while lowering risk. In simple terms, you need investments that don't all go up and down at the same time. Stocks and bonds used to go up and down at different times, but the ever increasing correlation of these two asset classes changed the amount of volatility experienced by portfolios.

As we looked at the amount of alternative investments in an endowment method portfolio, we identified that the effects of the non-correlation in combination with the superior returns of alternative investments contributed to the outperformance. This was a major breakthrough in concept for us. Not only did you want higher returns, but you wanted the returns to be non-correlated to stocks and even to bonds. What's more, you wanted the alternative investments to be non-correlated to each other. That is to say, each selected alternative investment should have non-correlation to other alternative investments.

There is a simple explanation of why this non-correlation works. When one of the selected investments is up, another is down. This provides both control over risk and an opportunity to create better returns. Most investors see the risk-reducing benefit of having something up and something down at the same time. The less evident part is how the energy of this movement is harnessed. To understand this added return potential, investors have to get over the notion that up is good and down is bad. If the investments selected tend to behave in an up and down pattern and not remain at the same price for long periods of time, then the movement can be converted to return through a simple rebalancing process. You can sell some of the ones that went up and buy more of the ones that went down. Essentially, you buy low and sell high.

An additional benefit was found in this investment method. The process of rebalancing was in reaction to what had already happened. It relied on changes in the non-correlated investments to continuously allow investors to "React" to the movements. Predicting the price movements of stocks, bonds, or markets was less important. Reacting through a rebalancing program took much of the importance of predicting away from the investment process.

This is a good time to recap the endowment method as designed for the average retail investor. The process starts with a good cash flow analysis. This allows longer cycle investments, especially alternatives, to be used to get potentially higher returns. Next, an investment policy is used to establish the percentages of each type of investment that is appropriate to the goals, risk tolerance, and time horizon for investment. From this policy, specific investments are selected to assure non-correlation across the portfolio, generally through alternative investments. The liquidity of alternative investments is maximized either through separate accounts (like institutions use) or through some other liquid form like non-correlated liquid alternative mutual funds or ETFs. Finally, the portfolio is rebalanced to sell some of the investments that went up and buy more of the investments that went down.

As you start to look at this method of investing, several curious features tend to emerge. The speed at which the investments go up and down (i.e., the frequency of their volatility) affect the investment return. How much the investments go up and down (i.e., the amplitude of their volatility) affect investment return. Investments that vary faster and higher, create more opportunity for rebalancing and more opportunity for return. This return produced by the variation of investment price relative to other investments I call Variation Alpha. It is not dependent on investments going up, but on the non-correlation effects of investment movement in a portfolio.

While reacting is the core process, predicting investment behavior is not eliminated with this approach. The prediction just changes. Instead of trying to predict direction of an investment price, the analysis focuses on understanding the conditions that create non-correlation of the investments. Just as stocks and bonds tended to correlate and go down at the same time in the financial crisis, alternative investments can be more correlated under certain conditions. I have found that this process of predicting non-correlation tends to be much easier than trying to call markets, though.

This process of creating a non-correlated alternative investment has been evolving over the past 30 years. Until 2006, very few of these non-correlated investments were available to investors who had less than $5 million in liquid investments (qualified purchasers). The laws affecting mutual funds changed, and by 2006, the structure to build an alternative mutual fund with low correlation was established. This made it possible for the average retail investor to access non-correlation in a liquid form, similar to the effects that separate accounts brought to institutions. By 2010, several companies had begun building non-correlated mutual funds giving investors daily liquidity.

The typical way that that alternative investments create non-correlation is by having some investments in the portfolio that benefit from price declines. The most common is the short position. This is where an investor benefits from the stock going down in price. The simplest way to understand this concept is with an example. Image you sell a stock at today's price and receive the cash. If you didn't own the stock you could borrow the shares from a lender with a promise to replace the shares later. If the price of the stock goes down, you could buy the share for less and give the lender the shares you borrowed. You got the cash at the higher price and paid the lender back at a lower price.

Short selling can be confusing at first, but the effect is to create benefit from the investment price going down. When you hold both a short position and a long position, the portfolio will have some parts that go up and some that go down. This is what long short alternative investment manager do to benefit from the price movement of stocks and limit the effects of the market movement on their decisions. When the amount of long and short positions completely eliminate the effects of the market, the portfolio is said to be "market neutral." Types of long and short positions in the portfolio determine how it will behave at different points in time. This is what creates the non-correlation behavior.

Bonds and bond derivatives can be used much the same way to create non-correlation in an alternative investment. In its simplest construction, the bond derivative creates an opposite price reaction to the bond. This allows for the bond manager to create as much or as little correlation to the bond market as the manager wants.

Many investment professionals don't believe that non-correlation is possible. When a chief investment officer (CIO) challenged me on the concept that all investments correlate under stress, I had to point out that I had yet to find a short position that correlated with a long position in a stock. He had to acknowledge that point as true. Then, I explained how some alternative investments used long and short investments in stocks to reduce correlation. He further acknowledged this to be true. Finally, I pointed to the types of investments that had low "net" exposure (longs minus shorts) as having very little correlation. While this CIO had very little experience or knowledge of alternative investment construction, I have found that this is more often the case with CIOs than you might expect. For such an important investment component in investment portfolios, you would think that knowledge of alternative investments to be a requirement to be a CIO. It would be like having a doctor who only knew about the right side of a body but nothing about the left side. Generally, CIOs generally rise to that position by being good at one type of investment strategy. Unless the CIO has been an alternative investment manager, he is less likely to understand how alternative investments are constructed.

You might ask why everyone wouldn't adopt this approach once they learn about it. It is used but the biggest and most successful endowments. It has a long track record of success. Smart hedge fund managers try to use it inside their portfolios to create absolute return. It would seem like this is an easy change to accept. On the contrary, one of the first things people do when they hear about this method of investing is to run to their current financial advisers and ask them what they think about it. Granted, there are many smart advisers out there, but it would be like asking a dentist about your neurosurgeon's recommendation. Yes, both the dentist and neurosurgeon work on the head, but have little knowledge of each other's professions. If even CIOs have difficulty understanding this investment method, the average adviser will generally have even less knowledge about constructing portfolios with alternative investments. The first reaction to something new often is to reject it. This is what I have seen from many advisers. They want to do what they know. Learning something new is often too time consuming and risks losing their current clients if adopted.

Additionally, this is a rather new approach for retail investors. Even though institutions have known about this approach for quite some time, the absolute return approach to investing didn't give the results of retail investor wanted during the bull market phase of an investment cycle. In time this will be less of an issue.

Refinements in the approach are continually evolving. After several quarters of experimenting with this approach, I have found that there are many ways that the level of energy captured from the movement can be improved. It reminds me of the progression of solar cells. At first you can capture some of the energy, but as the technology evolves, you find ways to increase the efficiency of the energy it captures. So too, the non-correlation method we use is continuously refined.

The most common question I get asked by investors is "How's your performance?" This is a valid question. Performance identifies the stress points and successes of a strategy. It identifies how much return is achieved for the level of risk taken. Like Malkiel and Brinson, my experience is primarily limited to observations. I can point to the endowment fund CIOs that use some version of non-correlation and the long-term performance advantage achieve by them (as much as 8+% better than the average retail investor); I can show a steady improvement in the performance of my clients' accounts, especially during volatile and down markets; and I can show how our hedge fund uses it to create pure alpha returns in a market neutral form. In 5-10 years from now, the "performance" question will have more meaning, but by that time, the damage may already be done to traditionally constructed portfolios. For many of my clients, it is enough to know that the smartest investors in the world at the best universities, who have little profit motivation to sell you something, have been using this method for more than 10-years with exceptional results.

Another question I get asked is "Why do I use this method?" I truly believe this will reduce the portfolio risk while giving opportunities to increase variation alpha over an investment cycle. If successfully implemented, the method is designed to produce better returns while keeping the portfolio risk at lower levels. Also, I like knowing that my clients sleep better at night during volatile markets because this method seeks to lower the up and down movements. I like seeing investors in this method experience higher returns at times they really need it. Most importantly, I like having an investment method that is designed to help people overcome economic and political stress that has created such unpredictability in the investment world and give them a tool to achieve their financial goals with greater certainty.

Let's review…
1. Non-correlated alternative investments can help reduce risk and improve returns when selected and used properly in a portfolio.
2. Rebalancing a portfolio of non-correlated investments takes the emotion out of the "buy low sell high" process.
3. The ability to construct this type of portfolio didn't exist for most retail investors until liquid alternative investments became available after the financial crisis of 2007-2009.
4. University endowments have been employing forms of this method for over 10 years with exceptional success.

I look at market volatility with a whole new perspective with this approach. A market that drops 15% is not a bad thing, but an opportunity to generate more variation alpha. Until now, the investment community has conditioned us to fear a market crash. If up is good and down is bad, then a market crash would be really bad. A non-correlated investment approach likes up and down behavior. As long as the securities selected have enough non-correlation, the opportunity for more return increases with markets that move rapidly.

Perhaps you have read about the market crash predictions that Ron Paul has been warning us will come in the coming years. He may be right. Much of what he says makes some sense. The problem with most market crash predictions is that the theory assumes that governments and companies cannot or will not react to the changes in the economy and markets. This simply isn't the case. Governments are willing to do much to prevent a recession or depression. That being said, if Ron Paul is right, what would happen to a non-correlated portfolio? Provided the non-correlation holds up, the likely increase in volatility would eventually allow for variation alpha to overcome the drop in market values experienced during the crash. While short-term declines in the portfolio would be likely, the long-term effects would be much less loss of portfolio value and the probable return to positive returns. A traditional portfolio is likely to have less protection as companies become weaker driving down both stock and bond values.

One of the reactions I hear to the Ron Paul message is "I'll just go to cash." With rising inflation and the dollar devaluation, cash becomes the least safe place for investment as its value depends on government stability, not profits of global companies. At least with shares of stock, the value remains the same relative to the economic conditions. Early 20th century Germany had a period of time where wheelbarrows of cash bought just one loaf of bread. If you had owned shares in the bakery, the value was relatively the same or higher given the demand for food and staples.

To implement and manage a non-correlated investment strategy requires a fair amount of effort. The strategy relies on trading (rebalancing) the positions to extract the variation alpha. This creates short-term gains and may be viewed by some as tax inefficient. I love putting the "no tax at any cost" investors in their place. I was a tax professional for 20 years. The decision to hold an investment or generate more gain is a math problem. The trading should create more net-of-tax gain than holding the investment and missing the opportunity to generate variation alpha. We have done the analysis, and it is hard to find a one-year period that didn't have better gains from rebalancing than a buy and hold strategy. With trading costs so low, we found that the rebalancing benefits were sustainable and persistent for most historical conditions and tax environments.

In summary, the ability to "React" instead of "Predict" makes investing less scary. This strategy is designed to reduce portfolio volatility and to profit from market declines. The "almost instantaneous and with no notice" market corrections don't have to be the accepted price of investing. Using this approach provides an option to the failing buy-and-hold strategies that worked up until 2000, and it provides a solution to the failing protection of a bond market that may be at the beginning of a long period of rising interest rates and declining bond prices.

Chapter 4 – Building Wealth Isn't Investing

"The greatest wealth is to live content with little."

Plato

"It is health that is real wealth and not pieces of gold and silver."

Mahatma Gandhi

"For what shall it profit a man, if he gain the whole world, and suffer the loss of his soul?"

Jesus Christ

"Health is the greatest gift, contentment the greatest wealth, faithfulness the best relationship."

Buddha

"For a successful entrepreneur it can mean extreme wealth. But with extreme wealth comes extreme responsibility. And the responsibility for me is to invest in creating new businesses, create jobs, employ people, and to put money aside to tackle issues where we can make a difference."

Richard Branson

At this point, we have seen that a predictive model for investing cannot be supported by academic studies. Essentially, it is gambling. A buy-and-hold method of investing has been failing to deliver acceptable returns since 2000. Bonds are at an all-time low for interest rates and have the risk of declining in value as interest rates rise. Cash investments (CDs, money markets, savings, etc.) no longer keep up with inflation. None of the traditional investments are good choices. The method of investing described in chapter 3 provides a possible solution as was shown by the outperformance achieved by the big endowment managers; however, even this method does not make the investor wealthy. It is designed to protect and grow investments to meet long-term goals given the current investment environment. So, the question remains, "How does one build wealth if not by investing?"

Building wealth is not the same as investing. Virtually every one of my clients got their wealth by some other means than investing. The investment process was simply a storage facility for their excess wealth. If you are going to your broker to get rich, consider this: If your broker had a way to get rich, wouldn't she be on her yacht enjoying life instead of managing your account? Maybe that's not a fair statement given the number of rich investment advisers willing to take your money into their strategies; however, most wealthy investment advisers got their wealth using other people's money, not by investing well.

There is a saying about the big brokerage firms, "They are good at taking their experience and your money to make it their money and your experience." The inexperienced investor may think that the brokers on Wall Street can make them rich, but the outcomes are often much different than the expectations. Brokers are there to sell investments. Their motivation is an investment sale, not the wealth of their clients. It is nice if both are achieved, but the goal is the sale of an investment. There are many caring financial advisers who seek their client's best interests, but the pressure of the investment houses to sell products is always there. Those brokers seeking to put their clients' best interests first are now migrating to the RIA platform where they have a fiduciary duty to their clients. In fact, the RIA structure for investment advice is growing rapidly and starting to become a viable competitor to the big brokers.

I admit that while my investment process appears to perform better over an investment cycle than most traditional predictive investment approaches, it is not designed to make my clients rich overnight. As I explain to my clients, I can help you build wealth by giving business and tax advice but I can help you preserve and grow it by helping you select better investments solutions. For my ultra-high net worth clients, I will save them more in taxes than I will likely make them in investment returns. When you consider that wealth generation is taxed at a 75-90% rate over a person's lifetime unless proper planning is done, it is hard to imagine making more than that in investment returns. If you don't believe me, consider the math. The wealthy who generate high-levels of ordinary income pay 40% federal income taxes and up to 10% in state income taxes. In addition, they pay a 6-9% sales tax, 1-4% in property taxes, and a variety of other taxes tacked onto purchases of items like communication services, utilities, and lodging. Even before the wealth builder has the privilege to pay those taxes, their corporations that generated the income paid 40% on the earnings to the federal government and up to 10+% to the state government. If the wealth builder still has money left over for investment, the investment earnings are taxed at a rate of 20-40% and the remaining balance at death gets taxed under the estate tax rules at 45% for federal and up to 17% for state. If any of the wealth is in an IRA, over 100% can be taxed at time of death.

So, why do so many people seek to get rich in the stock market? Probably the same reason so many people gamble. The odds might actually be a bit better at gambling, though. Playing the high-stakes, levered investment schemes that create the get-rich-quick strategies generally end in disaster. I had a friend who paid $2 million for sub-prime mortgages with a face value of almost $1 billion. He thought he was going to be rich, but he couldn't unload the securities, and the cost to collect the amounts owed on the mortgage debt was more than he could afford. It almost put him into bankruptcy (and in jail, but that's another story).

Predominantly, wealth building comes from effectively managing what you can control. Yes, some wealth is inherited or obtained by chance, but the majority comes from doing something that produces significantly more income than you spend. Control over the outcome is key to wealth building. Unlike investing, which either is done with some predictive science or through the reactive approach that I describe in this book, wealth building requires more control over the outcomes. The wealth builder identifies an activity that through their efforts and intelligence will yield profitable results.

Generically, I categorize the process of wealth building as running a businesses. The business may be 1) your career and personal brand (think famous CEO or entertainers), 2) your employer's brand (like a highly successful salesman), or 3) your own business brand (start-up businesses and innovators). Each of these three wealth-building approaches is a business. You need to have a product your target audience wants, market that product effectively, and bring in more revenue than it costs to build and sell the product. The process is the same whether marketing your own talents or that of your employer. Wealth builders own the process. They view the outcome as within their control. Once the formula starts to produce positive results, they find ways to accelerate the rate at which they can repeat the process.

For those managing their personal brand, this means having skills/knowledge others want, establishing demand for their services, and charging a rate that will build wealth. The business is selling their persona. Their public image and reputation is the business they run. Many of us opt for running someone else's business, but for those who want to market themselves, personal wealth can be built through effective marketing and management of their own personal brand.

Too often, we see those trying to promote their personal brands without taking the time to establish a skill or knowledge base that others desire. The numerous talent shows on television highlight these failed attempts to promote an unmarketable skill. Being the best at what you do takes time and effort, but it has to be suited to your physical limitations as well. If you are a 5' 0" slim 19 year old, you might think jockey instead of NBA center for your chosen skill. While the politically correct approach may encourage you to do what you love, wealth building through your personal brand requires a skill/knowledge that you can convert to a high rate of income. Failure is the most likely outcome unless you are honest and dedicated to your craft. It is perfectly acceptable to do what you love for little or no income, but not if your goal is to build wealth from it. Few have actually made large amounts of money on their lack of talent; however, talent is relative to the audience it reaches. Identifying the right audience can sometimes help. For example, the best soccer team wouldn't make nearly as much in the U.S.A. as they would playing in Europe or Latin America. The right audience makes all the difference.

The same principle goes for those building a business. The worst product in one market may be the best product in another. One of the wealthiest families I know built their initial wealth through taking something that was defective and finding a market that would accept the defects. The patriarch of this wealthy family grew up learning how to grade lumber. In the 1950s through the 1970s, builders required high-quality lumber for framing houses and other construction projects. When he discovered that the inferior-quality lumber was discarded, he arrange to buy it and resell it in Latin America where price was more important and lesser quality materials were accepted and used in construction. He found the right audience for what he had to sell.

It sometimes takes time to find the right venue for wealth building to take hold. Peter Druker, the famous professor of business management, noted that entrepreneurs learn from their failures. For many, success starts slow and builds over time, not unlike the compounding of interest in a savings account. University of Pennsylvania Assistant Professor Angela Lee Duckworth studies the psychological elements that influence success. As she notes in her Ted Talk, "who's going to earn the most money? ...[O]ne characteristic emerged as a significant predictor of success. And it wasn't social intelligence. It wasn't good looks, physical health, and it wasn't IQ. It was grit." Failing is not the problem. What you do with the failure determines your future success.

To sustain wealth, lifestyles must match the level of wealth created. We've all heard the unfortunate stories of athletes that depleted great sums of wealth through lavish lifestyles. Wealth can easily be lost, but is hard won. Steve Jobs, noted for his under-stated lifestyle, said, "Bottom line is, I didn't return to Apple to make a fortune. I've been very lucky in my life and already have one. When I was 25, my net worth was $100 million or so. I decided then that I wasn't going to let it ruin my life. There's no way you could ever spend it all, and I don't view wealth as something that validates my intelligence." This attitude that wealth was incidental to those things that mattered to him drove Steve Jobs to make his entire life an amazing adventure that allowed him to be the best at what he did. His modest lifestyle was just one form of expressing the attitude he took that ultimately made him the legend he has become.

The largest fortunes were often built by the most frugal people. One of my wealthiest clients still visits second-hand stores and stays on a strict personal budget. Doris Duke, one of the wealthiest women of the 20th century, was said to do the same thing, buying many of her clothes and personal items at the thrift shop. I am not advocating that personal spending be this far below one's wealth levels, but the attitude of preserving and growing wealth is key to virtually every wealth-building effort. Finding the balance between spending and investing is key to enjoying the fruits of one's labor for many years to come.

So, what is the relationship between wealth building and investing? By its very nature, wealth building relies on investing as the storehouse for the profits harvested. In its broadest sense, investing includes non-interest bearing cash holdings, not just stocks and bonds. Even if profits are kept under a mattress in hard currency, the wealth builder would be making an investing decision with those holdings. Investing is the process of allocating excess funds to achieve a rate of return (even if zero or negative) that the investor accepts as fair for the risk taken. Sometimes we accept that a zero return is acceptable. In certain investments we even expect a negative return in early years. This is known as a "J-Curve" return because of the shape formed when plotting the annual returns of the investment. Higher risk investments, like certain private equity funds, have this expected decline in the first few years.

Those moving from wealth building to investing decisions often get the two confused. I've heard clients complain that they get a higher return from their business activities than the returns from their investment portfolios. This actually should be the case. If the business activity isn't producing a higher return, something may be failing in the business. If investments are producing higher returns, than the investments may be taking too much risk to ensure long-term wealth preservation.

Should wealth builders reinvest proceeds back into their businesses? Initially, this may be a sound idea. At some point, the excess profits need to be set aside to lay off the risk of business failure. Investing the excess profits gives the business reserves for the unexpected. It creates opportunities for growth of new profit centers. Most importantly, it helps secure the success of the wealth building efforts through diversifying the risk and income streams. Through a systematic approach to balancing risk and return, wealth building allocates to both the business and investing activities. Failure to do both elevates the risk of failure.

Investing comes in two forms – liquid and illiquid. Initially, business owners should use liquid investments to balance out the higher risk and more illiquid business investment. As investment levels grow relative to the business value, investors should consider whether illiquid investments need to play a role in their portfolios. To explain the reason for using illiquid investments, consider the typical bank certificate of deposit (CD). The longer you let the bank have your money, the higher the rate of return they pay you. A two-year CD pays a higher rate than a one-year CD. The more illiquid, the higher the rate. Other investments often work the same way. For example, if you lock up your investment capital for 7-10 years in a private equity real estate fund, you expect to receive a higher rate of return from that investment than something with daily liquidity like a publicly traded real estate stock.

We all have heard, "Cash is King." Initial wealth-building efforts should remember this rule. Until you have enough cash, avoid locking up your investment capital for long periods of time. A ready war chest of cash makes it possible to "buy when others are selling and sell when others are buying," a sound principle of value investing often quoted by Sir John Templeton, one of the most successful value investors. The advantages of cash are far reaching in the wealth-building process; however, the loss of investment return from cash that is not employed needs to be balanced against the excess returns achieved by the opportunistic use of the cash.

Social consciousness dictates that we discuss the impact wealth building has on the world as a whole. Many wealthy people often feel a sense of guilt as a bi-product of their success. They question if it is morally right to have so much when others have so little. One of my greatest joys comes from helping my wealthy clients develop a sound philanthropy plan that involves them and their children in the process of helping others. In this effort, the guilt they once felt often is replaced by joy and a peaceful spirit of caring.

Typical arguments against wealth building come from the assumption that there are limited resources in the world that need to be shared fairly. The other side of this argument is that wealth building is a great motivator to elevate the living standard of an entire society as new recourses are created by these efforts. Despite the popular rhetoric heard, I believe both sides of the argument desire to see poverty and suffering eliminated and to empower people to be productive contributors to their communities. The common thread of both the wealthy and the poor is the desire to meet their physical and emotional hierarchy of needs. This desire is the basis of human motivation. Rather than one class bringing another down so that they can rise, the goal should be to raise all people to a higher level. This avoids conflict and acknowledges the common goals we all have for our lives and those of our families.

Recent awareness about the global impacts of certain types of wealth- building activities raise additional concerns including environmental effects, contributions to violence and conflicts, and health effects. These and other concerns make for great political debate over the benefits and evils of capitalism, socialism, and various hybrid forms employed by governments the world over; however, it is the beliefs each of us hold about the causes for these social ills that drive us to seek specific solutions – solutions that are often very offensive to others with differing belief systems.

For example, when making a choice about feeding certain

populations in Africa, is it better to use natural farming techniques and let current populations starve due to poor crop production or use genetically modified seeds and chemical farming techniques to triple output for the local populations? While infrastructure projects such as roads and rail systems would solve many of the food needs of these populations, projects like those take years to implement. Our belief systems drive our response to this problem. Some may say the introduction of GMO crops has long-term impacts that are not worth the benefit derived in the short run. Yet, that is hard to hear if your child is dying of malnutrition.

Investors are inevitably linked to wealth builders through their investment choices. A wealth builder who seeks public capital must live with the outcomes of the public investment decisions. A rapidly growing investment trend is that of "Impact Investing." This form of investing attempts to express investors' values in their investment choices. Investors actively seeks to reward wealth builders that exhibit greater awareness and participation in the solutions that they believes will make for a better society. Unlike socially responsible investing which avoids certain investments, impact investing actively invests in targeted companies.

The application of impact investing can be harmonious with the non-correlated investing strategies in this book. While a limited number of alternative investments are currently available that include impact investing, hedge fund managers that manage money for many E.U. and some U.S. institutions are required to have investment policies to avoid investing in the securities of major offending companies, municipalities, and countries. The hedge fund (and by extension, liquid alternative mutual funds and ETFs) provides the perfect vehicle to express a social opinion by being able to invest capital in the desired securities and sell short the undesired. This allows for the fund's investors to gain from promoting "good" behavior as well as benefit from driving the "bad actors" out of business.

Disregard for the poor and marginalized is often the biggest complaint I hear about wealth-building activities. Complaints include gentrification of cities, elimination of community resources, and relocation of jobs and educational opportunities. I will leave it to the wealth builder to decide how to use the wealth created, but civilized governments will step in to help their populations and use resources from those that have to help those in need. Wealth builders should be aware of their collective responsibility and the economic benefit from directly solving the social issues rather than relying on governments to force a solution. Hedge fund groups like Hedge Funds Care and the Robin Hood Foundation are good examples of positive collective responses by the wealthy hedge fund managers seeking to help and empower those of lesser means.

On a personal note, I would love to see a world where governments were driven out the business of providing welfare because individuals (not governments) with the means to do so were responsible and caring enough to eliminate poverty, hunger, and the effects of misfortune. If no one qualified for governmental assistance because they had enough private assistance, the national treasuries wouldn't need to be tapped to support entitlement programs. Unfortunately, there will always be those who need help and too few willing to help them without encouragement from their governments, churches, and communities. True wealth comes from the way we live our lives, not from the size of our bank accounts. Having the means to support our efforts to help each other is the greatest blessing of all. That being said, let's examine the wealth-building process in more detail.

Understanding the difference between wealth building and investing is key to building a successful plan to reach your financial goals. Relying on your financial adviser to make up for your lack of wealth-building success is not a sound plan. Using your financial planners and wealth advisers to help calculate and set appropriate lifestyle levels and identify sustainable investment strategies gives you the greatest chance of meeting the financial requirements of your personal goals. In the end, wealth building is not investing. Wealth building is about running a business – the business of you, the business you own, or the business you promote. Learning how to succeed in these business-building efforts takes hard work, a bit of luck, and a lot of grit.

Once achieved, wealth is not about having a lot of money, but about what money means to you in living the best life you can live. Unfortunately, the majority of the world sees wealthy people as generally unworthy and uncaring. Yet, even the critics want improvement in their own financial situation. It seems ironic that most people generally want wealth but describe wealthy people as "bad." Our competitive nature to survive and thrive drives these views as does our definition of wealthy. It creates a financial divide that is hard to span beyond a one-on-one relationship. Class systems always seem to emerge along these wealth lines, even in a democratic society. It spawns resentment and envy between classes. Politicians use this to foment unrest and win votes and support. Media groups get higher ratings by highlighting the differences between economic classes and playing to their viewers' biases.

One of the hardest parts of being wealthy is the lack of empathy and concern that others have for the wealthy. Building a stress-free wealth plan goes beyond the numbers. It means understanding how to live a satisfying life. The friend that once used to console you may become envious of you. Finding an understanding friend who can share your pain and joys becomes increasingly difficult. Many with wealth start to question the motivation of those around them. "Is it my money or me that they like," becomes the concern. The essential human need to be loved becomes much more difficult to feel, if not find, for the wealthy.

Despite these drawbacks from wealth, a satisfying life can be lived. For many, helping others becomes their joy. Bill and Malinda Gates, the richest couple in the world for many years, gave the majority of their wealth to their charitable foundation. Finding a purpose that transcends this life and lives on through those they touch gives meaning to those who have built wealth. This lack of love felt in the loneliness of wealth is often satisfied by expressing love and compassion to other humans who live in desperate conditions. Unweighting the burden of wealth to unweight the burden of poverty in another person creates an inner peace that is hard to replicate through living an extravagant lifestyle.

As wealth builds, many come to need the experience of charitable acts. This emotional need is counter intuitive to years of generating and amassing wealth. The expectation of pleasure from wealth alone is replaced by a need to find emotional connection with others. Each stage of the wealth process comes with new opportunities and new emotions. Understanding this journey of wealth building is essential to the long-term success of the effort.

As you build a financial plan for your future, remember to include both wealth building and investing in the plan. Acknowledge the differences and accept the distinct role each plays in managing the risks and successes of achieving your financial goals. Don't look to your investments to make you rich, and don't fear taking control of your financial future in your wealth building plans. Identify that which will give you success through your efforts and combine it with a lifestyle and investment plan that is well thought out. In this combination, you will have the highest chance of living the life many of you only dreamed was possible.

Chapter 5 – The Age of Conflict

"I am more concerned about the return of my money than the return on my money."
Mark Twain

Investors have responded to the 2007-2009 financial crisis by holding cash as their dominant asset even though cash, after taxes, has not kept up with inflation during the period 1926-2012 (Russ Koesterich, BlackRock Global Chief Investment Strategist, Market Realist, Sep 22, 2014). This behavior is expected after the big declines in stocks that the world experienced. Bonds, while initially falling in value, still produced positive returns during every calendar year of the financial crisis. It wasn't until 2013 that bonds (measured by Barclays Aggregate) actually went negative for a full calendar year, but investors seem to not be taking a chance on either stocks or bonds. Cash has become king. Why would cash be so important to investors?

According to the 2014 study on peace in the world conducted by the Institute for Economics and Peace (IEP), "the world as a whole has been getting incrementally less peaceful every year since 2008." This study shows that only 11 countries are free from conflict. The study further estimates these conflicts to cost the world $9.8 trillion or 11.3% of global GDP. One can't help but notice the correlations of rising cash reserves and world conflicts rising. It only makes sense that Investors around the world would get more liquid in the face of political and military conflict, but does this have any effect on the markets? Surprisingly, it doesn't seem to have the same effect as one would expect.

The measure of risk in a market is its volatility. While there are many types of investment risk, I am only concerned about volatility for this discussion. Typically, investors follow a volatility index called the VIX to see how this volatility is changing. At the close of 2014, the VIX trend line is at a level less than half that of May 2009, the beginning of the post crisis recovery. Even though conflicts are rising in most countries around the world, volatility is dropping. To understand this behavior, the investor population needs to be identified to see who is actually doing the investing and why they wouldn't be worried about conflict.

"The biggest source of fresh cash in American equities isn't speculators or exchange-traded funds -- it's companies buying their own stock, by a 6-to-1 margin...Companies in the S&P 500 have spent more than $2 trillion on their own stock since 2009, underpinning an equity rally in which the index has more than tripled." Joseph Ciolli, Lu Wang, and Oliver Renick, Bloomberg News, March 4, 2015. The corporate buy-back programs are fueling the majority of flows into equities. Essentially, the rise in stock market has been due to companies using financial engineering to increase their own stock price. It isn't the investing public showing more confidence in the companies and the economies supporting them.

I will get into the detail on corporate buyback programs in the next chapter, but the impact on stock price is the point that is being made here. The average investor is stockpiling cash. The corporate investor is buying back its own stock. Neither the individual nor the institution want to invest in the stock market. Both are essentially investing in themselves.

For individual investors, their reluctance to spend or invest is based on their view of the world. One measure of this individual sentiment is the University of Michigan's U.S. Consumer Sentiment Index. While no index measure is a definitive statement on an economy or stock market, it can give some insight on behavioral patterns to help understand the reasons people do the things they do. This index shows that the confidence levels, while trending upward since 2011, have not averaged levels experienced even during the bursting of the tech bubble. That's right. On average, the U.S. consumer felt better about things during the tech bubble crash then they do now, even though the S&P 500 is at an all-time high. Essentially, we trust ourselves (buy back our company stock or wait on the sideline in cash) but not the market as a whole.

While cash has been the dominant asset class, retail investors have made two distinctive moves in their portfolios in 2015. First, they have been moving to lower-cost ETF index funds from mutual funds. Second, they are moving out of fixed income to equities, especially hedged European equities. An interesting sub-story is that institutions are moving out of equities, especially U.S. equities. To follow this, just look at the flows into Vanguard's S&P 500 and Total Stock Market, the low cost ETFs preferred by retail investors, and compare it to the flows out of SPDR S&P 500 and the PowerShares QQQ, preferred by institutions for large-cap investing in the U.S. stock market. In typical fashion, the retail investors are late to the party. This behavior has been seen before the last two market crashes. Returns of the market appear to be drawing cautious retail investors away from cash and bonds just in time to let institutions sell out and let retail investors absorb the brunt of the downturn.

Even with all this movement into equities in 2015, worldwide, cash was at a 7-month high at the end of May 2015. While retail investors in the U.S. are adding equities, investors in many other countries worldwide are reducing their equity holdings. In the UK, equity holdings are at the lowest allocation percentage since the August 2012 EU debt crisis. Some of this may be due to the strengthening dollar against EU currencies in the first quarter of 2015, but this trend reversed in the second quarter.

Investors continue to feel that cash, even if paying less than inflation, is better than taking a risk on bonds and stocks. As investor sentiment continues to erode around the world, investors continue to believe that the preservation of capital is more important than the hope of a better return in the capital markets.

Finding ways to better control the investment outcome has led to a rise in cash reserves and other investment solutions. In particular, the private equity investment has become more popular and has given investors a better return on average. Private equity is the investing in non-public companies. These are companies that do not have a listing of their stock on a public stock exchange. As such, the stock of these companies are not being monitored every second of the day with CEOs and their CFOs defending the stock price with every quarterly financial report.

At times, the average return of private equity companies has been nearly double the stock market returns. It is no wonder that private equity investing, particularly in the creation of small businesses, has been trending upward. At least these companies are outside of the big banks' control. Investors are looking for a better emotional connection to the investment as well as some sense of direct control and involvement. While investment banks continue to dominate private equity investment activity, more direct investment opportunities are emerging. Investment banks layer on fees that investors are starting to question the value proposition. For the ultra-high net worth, direct and co-investment into private equity at a much lower expense ratio has become an appealing alternative to the private equity fund. This sidesteps the investment bank fees for pooling private investment into a fund made available only to qualified purchasers. Additionally, it allows for the company receiving the investment to avoid the pressure for immediate growth that investment banks and big private equity promoters demand from the company. Business strategies of these private companies can follow longer-cycle plans that often result in better outcomes for both sustainable profits and community responsibility.

The rise of the crowd-funding solution and the emergence of the baby boomer small business are two examples of this trend. As an example, the new 3 World Trade Center was partially crowdfunded. Many of the new technology companies are seeking crowdfunding. This trend to find more control and better outcomes from their investment dollar shows no sign of slowing, either. Research firm, Massolution, found that crowdfunding grew by 167% in 2014 and raised over $16 billion worldwide. Over half of the funds raised in 2014 were in the USA. Growth is expected to continue. Interestingly, the royalty-based crowd funding solution was the fastest growing. This approach allows the investor to participate in the revenue stream and lets business management worry about controlling the expenses. Profit participation often puts management into the position of competing with investors for a share of the revenue (i.e., management for salaries and investors for dividends). This royalty-based approach seems to have a fresh appeal that is better at aligning the investment return to the success of the concept. It also drives better behavior by management as they get more reward for good expense control.

Will investors return to public markets, or will private equity be a long-cycle trend driven by the populist desire to reverse the years of corporate raiding and profit taking by large banks and tycoons? Certainly, movements like Occupy Wall Street reflect a growing public disappointment in the current system. Effective solutions to these problems require both regulatory and legislative support. The Jobs Act, which brought in the crowdfunding possibility in the USA, and the associated regulatory framework for its implementation seem to be helping meet the public's need for another investment solution. Be prepared, though. Big investment banks will not let go easily. Private equity profits are just too high. The trend will likely be met with some resistance. Fraud and poorly conceived investment opportunities will emerge in the crowdfunding space. This will generate concerns that only the larger investment banks will claim to be able to solve. "Protect the Public" will once again be the rally cry that drives these types of grassroots movements into the hands of the large corporations who claim to know better and have the resources to do the job the right way. In some cases, larger corporations may be a more efficient solution, but teasing out the fair solution will be the heavy lifting that comes with changes like this.

Chapter 6 – The Self-Indulgent Company

"Growth for the sake of growth is the ideology of the cancer cell."

Edward Abbey

Lu Wang, and Oliver Renick (BloombergBusiness, March 3, 2015) describes companies as "in love with themselves." The article goes on to say "Stock buybacks, which along with dividends eat up sums of money equal to almost all the Standard & Poor's 500 Index's earnings, vaulted to a record in February [2015], with chief executive officers announcing $104.3 billion in planned repurchases. That's the most since TrimTabs Investment Research began tracking the data in 1995 and almost twice the $55 billion bought a year earlier." This truly is the era of corporate buybacks, but when did this era begin?

The debate is certainly active on the causes of the trend, but many analysts see the changes occurring in the early to mid-1970s. This coincides with the economic pressure the U.S. experienced as previously described. Are corporate buyback programs the natural result of boards trying to keep shareholders happy in the face of mounting pressure on profits? Are company boards manipulating the stock price through periodic price-supports of buyback programs? Questions an investor would want answered if they had to pick stocks and call markets in order to create investment returns. At a minimum, it creates doubt in the minds of many investors as to the fairness of the playing field for stock investors.

According to Louis Cammarosano in an article published in Inman on March 2, 2015, "Corporations seek higher returns and react to artificially low rates by buying back their own shares (either with existing cash or with dollars borrowed at the artificially low rates) to reduce the inventory of shares available on the market and thereby increase their earnings per share. As earnings per share increase, a company's stock price rises." Cammarosano goes on to say, "Any increase in interest rates may have a devastating effect on the stock market. This will make the Fed reluctant to reverse its six-year, zero-interest-rate policy failure and start raising rates."

The case is laid out by many that this low-rate environment has the effect of rewarding bad behavior in companies. When the element of risk is removed, as measured by the rate borrowers pay, those lending money suffer and those borrowing profit. If the government is the lender, they may be faced with collecting bad loans. While low rates may be one stimulus for the buyback programs, the previous record year for corporate buybacks was in 2007 before rates began to fall. Something else is certainly going on here, not just low rates.

"Corporate profitability is not translating into widespread economic prosperity. The allocation of corporate profits to stock buybacks deserves much of the blame... and in the short term buybacks drive up stock prices," concludes William Lazonick, Harvard Business Review, and September 2014. Lazonick believes the increase in stock compensation of CEOs encouraged this behavior, but what are the facts on CEO stock compensation?

According to the Equilar 2014 CEO Pay Strategies Report, "The years since 2009 have seen performance-based equity take center stage with the share of S&P 1500 CEOs receiving it rising from 39.7% to 63.8%. Performance-based equity is even more popular within the S&P 500, received by 75.7% of CEOs." It is a simple formula, the higher the stock price, the richer the CEOs get. What isn't as simple is seeing the effects of buybacks on productivity and wealth-building in the U.S.

Reading further in Lazonick's report, he demonstrates that "From 1948 to the mid-1970s, increases in productivity and wages went hand in hand. Then a gap opened between the two." Again, be careful not to confuse correlation with causation. There may be other forces at work than the simple greed of CEOs.

Let's take a look at how company governance works to better understand the way buyback programs get started. Companies are governed by boards and owned by investors (shareholders, unit holders, partners, etc., hereafter referred to as just "shareholders"). A board hires the CEO to run the company. Boards represent the investor, and CEOs answer to the board. Boards determine CEO compensation. If a board makes stock price the basis for judging a CEO's performance, CEOs will respond by driving up stock price. So, are boards to blame for this?

Boards are elected by shareholders. Certain shareholders hold more voting power than others in the process of electing board members. This gives large shareholders more control over who is on the board. In not a few cases, the CEO is a major shareholder in the company. This gives the CEO power over who is on the board. In other words, the CEO can control who sets his/her compensation. Not a good thing for the rest of the shareholders.

In the majority of cases, institutional investors (pensions, endowments, foundations, mutual funds, hedge funds, ETFs, etc.) are the primary shareholders of the stock. These institutions buy the stock hoping it will go up through good management and a favorable market. The institutions are primarily driven by investment committees and chief investment officers (CIOs) who directly influence investment committee decisions. For the most part, the investment committees want the stock price to go up to provide a better pension, bigger endowment payment, expanded charitable activity, or higher fund performance. All the way up the ladder, from CEO to shareholder, the motivation has become a higher stock price.

The first lesson I learned working in the Finance department of Merrill Lynch was that the metric you used to judge the manager (and set his/her compensation) determined the behavior. When Stan O'Neal become CFO, he changed the divisional metric from Return on Equity (ROE) to Pre-tax Margin (PTM). Now, ROE favored the Private Client business (retail brokers) and PTM favored the division in which Stan had worked, the Institutional business (trading and investment banking). This simple change made it possible to move the focus of the firm to trading and investment banking and away from Private Client. The retail brokerage and the asset management businesses became less important to the company under this new metric. In the end, it was this move that allowed more resources of Merrill Lynch to be placed on risky trading of mortgages and ultimately forced its sale to Bank of America. When profit became the most important metric, the long-term use of equity capital became less important. ROE was measured over longer periods of time. Profit was measured on a quarterly reporting cycle. It may be easy to blame Stan for this change and its effect on Merrill Lynch, but he was responding to board pressure on the then CEO of Merrill Lynch, David Kamanski, to improve Merrill Lynch stock price relative to companies like Morgan Stanley and Charles Schwab. Stan's plan worked, at least in the short run. It just came with a big "tail risk" that eventually sank the company.

With shareholders, boards, and CEOs all wanting higher stock prices, the quarterly reporting of earnings becomes the main focus. This is a bit like teaching to the test in schools. Everyone may get the right answer, but there is no understanding of how to produce or sustain value for the long-term. This focus is not innately wrong. Profits support a company and its employees. Without profits in our big companies, a lot of people would be without jobs. The focus "only" on profit to obtain stock price creates a lack of long-term planning. When stock prices fall because a CEO invests in long-term productivity, the board (and activist shareholders) react by questioning the value of such moves and sometimes punish the CEO for this behavior. Corporate buybacks may just be a response to this punishment or implied punishment.

Corporate buybacks come with a price. Where did the money come from to buy back the stock? Typically, it comes from two sources, profits and debt. If the source is profit, the company is effectively saying to the shareholders "We know better how to manage your profits than you do." That's fine unless the shareholders expected that dividends would be part of their investment experience in that stock. Even if the shareholders did not expect dividends from the company, the use of cash to buy back stock can increase the leverage of the balance sheet (a higher debt to equity ratio).

This concept of leverage is very important to understand. Just like a mechanical lever, the more you slide the lever to one side or the other of the pivot point, the more the impact the long side can have on the short side. Think about using a board to lift a heavy rock. You jam the board under the rock and pivot the board on a support close to the rock in order to allow for you to gain a mechanical advantage over the weight of the rock. This is where the risk of a market supported by leverage becomes more important. So long as prices go up, leverage is good. When prices start to go down, the downward impact is even greater because of the leverage. If $6 to every $1 of new money in the stock market comes from corporate buybacks, what happens when the CFOs decide that prices will be declining and they need to "de-lever" their balance sheets? Will they want to sell some of that stock they purchased back to the market and pay off some of their debt? What will happen to stock prices when there are more sellers than buyers? Economics 101 taught us that this imbalance, more supply than demand, results in a drop in price until the number of buyers and sellers equalizes. This de-levering effect could accelerate a downward market more than if corporations didn't engage in this financial engineering.

Using debt is no different. If the source of cash for a corporate buyback is company debt, the balance sheets of the companies are leveraged to make this possible. In June 2012, the central banks around the world decided that a global financial disaster could be avoided by working together to offer cheap loans to countries and companies who needed help. The rate would no longer be tied to the risk of repayment. Governments and their central banks would effectively guarantee the loans until the economies got better and the financial crisis was over. This made it possible for companies to get an ever increasing amount of cheap debt, even if they didn't need it. Central banks had to make the offer so enticing that countries and companies would not say no. Effectively, the rate was zero. Companies took the loans and put it on their balance sheets. Corporations also found that issuing bonds into the public markets was easy and cheap. This allowed them to extend the date they would need to pay back their debt and give them more time than the short-term central bank loans to make repayment.

Just like the mortgage models that assumed real estate would always go up, these buyback models assume that the company can always keep the price of its stock going up by buying more stock and borrowing more money to do so. It sounds a lot like the scheme developed by Ponzi and made even more famous by Madoff. Once the music stops, we will see who no longer has a chair. Just like most self-indulgent activities, those who take it to excess tend to self-destruct. What's worse is that many retail investors will have placed their bets on a market bubble that the insiders will have already abandoned.

With each market crash since 2000 getting ever bigger, the next crash has the potential to be more devastating than any seen since 1929. The crash will likely have the largest amount of corporate buybacks flowing back into the market at the worst possible time. The tech bubble and financial crisis had much stronger governments and consumer balance sheets. The next market crash comes with historically high government debt and dramatically reduced consumer resilience. I have only found one possible solution while we wait for this prophetic calamity. A highly effective non-correlated investment strategy is the only approach that removes the fear of dramatic losses and gives a potential to profit from the volatility of market crashes.

Chapter 7 – The Fall of Hedge Funds

"Pride goes before destruction, a haughty spirit before a fall."
Proverbs 16:18, The New International Version Bible

The hedge fund index underperformed the S&P 500 every year from 2009 through 2014. Warren Buffett and George Sorros both declared that hedges funds cannot beat the market. The hedge fund is dead! Or is it? In this chapter, I examine what defines a good hedge fund, how to use hedge strategies in a non-correlated portfolio, and why alternative investments, like hedge funds, continue to have a place in investment portfolios. I also show some of the tricks that some hedge fund managers have used to try and deceive you and why hedge funds got such a bad reputation after the financial crisis.

Part of the problem of human language is that words mean different things to different people. Saying that hedge funds cannot beat the market is rather self-deprecating for Buffett and Sorros who are known as the best hedge fund managers of all time. In a way, they are saying that "they" can no longer beat the market. That's fine for Sorros who only manages his own money, but Buffett continues to ask for outside investor money to be placed with him. Is Mr. Buffett saying he is no longer a good investment?

Before we examine this question about the future of hedge funds, it may be good to review what a hedge fund is and does. There are many definitions of hedge funds, but I will use the one from the Managed Funds Association – "A private investment pool, managed by a professional investment firm." This classic definition has three parts – 1. Private, 2. Pool, and 3. Professional Investment Firm.

It was long thought that a hedge fund was a private fund with no public registration. This allowed the manager of the fund to keep much of his "secret sauce" out of the view of the public. Hedge funds no longer have as much privacy as before because of a) the rise of liquid alternative funds, b) a public version of hedge funds, and c) the reporting requirements of new laws like Dodd Frank. The use of the word "Private" to describe a hedge fund is far less true than just 10 years ago.

Hedge funds were defined as a pool of money. The pooling of funds for investment by more than one investor has long been a way to manage money and is primarily regulated by the Investment Company Act of 1940. Pooling in a private fund requires that the investors be "sophisticated," "accredited," and sometimes "qualified." Each of these terms have specific meaning and are defined so that private funds pre-qualify the investor before engaging in discussions about the strategy and making an investment in the fund. Now that liquid alternative mutual funds have become more common, the hedge strategies of private funds can sometimes be found in publicly registered mutual funds in the USA or UCITS in other parts of the world. Investors no longer need to meet the requirements of sophistication, accreditation, or qualified purchaser when buying a publicly registered fund.

Pooling had certain benefits for the investors. It allowed the fixed costs of running a fund to be spread over more investors, and it provided greater incentives for the best managers to leave their high-paying jobs to run the private fund. Additionally, a large pool of money made it possible to use certain strategies that depended on large investment purchases. For example, if you need to buy an investment for $100 million, a pooled investment made it possible for the investor with $2 million to join the private investment pool and benefit from the strategy.

Finally, a hedge fund has been defined as professionally managed. This distinguishes is from investment clubs. The manager gets paid a fee for the management of the pool. Charging investment fees is a regulated activity. After the 1929 crash, the US government put several laws in place to protect the investing public. One of those laws made sure investment advisers were properly trained and filed certain reports with the SEC. Hedge funds were exempt from much of that registration process until the Dodd Frank regulations of 2010 sought to better align hedge funds with traditional investment advisory firms. Now most hedge funds have SEC registered investment advisory firms that charge a management fee to the hedge fund investors.

Hedge funds experienced fairly significant changes in the aftermath of the financial crisis. Even though the hedge fund index went down much less than the equity markets and recovered much quicker to the levels before the downturn, the index itself has underperformed relative to the equity market broad indexes. Part of the reason for the underperformance is the time period measured. Looking strictly on a calendar year basis, the hedge fund index has underperformed the equity market from 2009-2014. Looking over a longer period, hedge funds returns still look fairly competitive to the equity markets.

So, why would Mr. Buffett think that hedge funds are no longer a better investment than the market? In the aftermath of the 2007-2009 financial crisis, the governments around the world needed to make decisions to save their banking systems, financial markets, and economic engines of prosperity. Each government had its own issues to solve, but most developed countries knew that the plan needed three phases – 1) stabilize, 2) stimulate, and 3) support. The stabilizing efforts included the government buying private mortgages, and certain company equity, and the forced consolidation of companies to spread the pain to financially stronger areas of the private sector. The stimulus included monetary policy to pump cheap money into the economy and fiscal policy to help companies keep more of their profits for recovery purposes. The support phase included policy changes to reduce systemic risks that led to the crisis and increased monetary stimulus to enable economic growth.

These recovery efforts led to changes in the way the financial markets reacted to risk. By working together, the central banks and their governments created an environment where risk was no longer rewarded. The very reason hedge funds existed, to hedge risk while seeking more reward, had effectively been eliminated. To understand this relationship, the debt markets demonstrate the relationship best.

If a borrower does not have good credit, the loan has a higher probability of not being paid back. This potential loss is offset by lenders charging a higher interest rate. The additional interest is meant to offset these losses across the lenders loan portfolio and normalize the profit it makes on all of its loans.

When a central bank says that is will pay for any bad loans, this risk of a bad loan goes away and the interest rates can be lower as a result. After the financial crisis, the central banks wanted commercial banks to loan money to get companies back in business. This was done by backstopping loan losses and making it possible for consumers and businesses to borrow money even if they had a low credit rating. This was meant to pump money into the economies around the world and get the economic engine started.

In the early years, 2009-2011, the efforts to stabilize the economies worked well in stronger countries, but was failing in some of the weaker economies. In the summer of 2012, two central banks decided to work together to give one last boost of stimulus through programs called "quantitative easing" in the U.S.A. and "bond buyback" in the EU. This helped stop the "contagion" thought to exist if certain countries had economic failures.

Consequently, how did these recovery efforts hurt hedge funds? Before 2007, hedge funds would evaluate where risk of certain investments was too low or too high relative to the efficient frontier (the market average rate of return for a given amount of risk). This evaluation enabled them to short the low risk (too much return for the risk) and go long the high risk (too little return for the risk) knowing that the market forces would bring the returns back in line with the risk at some point. If low risk and high risk investments have the same return because of monetary and fiscal policies, the advantage of a long/short strategy are significantly reduced if not eliminated.

The main drivers of traditional hedge fund performance were effectively eliminated by these economic recovery and stimulus policies. The "smart" hedge fund managers recognized this dislocation of risk and took advantage of it by using leverage and other techniques to extract outsized returns for their investors. The majority of hedge fund managers continued to try and extract value from the risk/reward models they had always used. As a result, the hedge fund indexes reflected the average manager who was paying for insurance (the hedge) when it was not needed. This added cost of investing dampened returns relative to the world equity markets and led to the underperformance hedge funds have experienced.

Will hedge funds continue to show underperformance? Once risk matters again, the models that extract returns from dislocation of risk and reward are likely to work better than a normal equity market; however, this statement must be qualified to include the recognition that the instantaneous market adjustments that a computerized trading environment presents is much different than the more manual environment that existed in pre-2007 equity markets. As such, it will be increasingly difficult to find predictable dislocations of risk/return that can be realize as outperformance. It is more likely that the funds that extracted returns from structural and behavioral imperfections will be the more successful funds and the risk/return game will gradually become a way to just dampen the extreme volatility of returns, not to generate any outperformance.

This brings up the next topic about the role of hedge funds in a portfolio. When asked what hedge funds do for a portfolio, the novice investor generally thinks that the hedge fund should generate a higher return than the market. This concept of hedge funds generating a higher return comes from the press immortalizing the legendary managers that have done this. The public, and the press by extension, do not get excited about a hedge fund manager that gets half the return of the market at a quarter of the risk. Investors want performance even to the point of chasing it. As long as they can tolerate the ups and downs, the higher return approach can do better over certain time periods.

The first problem of using higher performing portfolios is aligning the time period for investing with the time period for spending the investment. Retirees understand this relationship better than any other investor. The retiree knows that they need to spend their profits. Selling at a loss and spending that money locks in the loss forever. If a portfolio is down 30% and is sold off to support the needs of the investor, the investor will never get a chance to recover that loss. Higher performing portfolios generally have more risk, and, accordingly, can go down more than less risky portfolios. For this reason, many financial planners lower the risk of retiree portfolios to avoid having to sell at a loss.

The second problem of chasing performance is the effect downturns have on investor behavior. As a portfolio goes down, investors can feel like the downturn is just too great to continue the ride. This discomfort can result in a "sell low" behavior that locks in the loss and removes the participation in the recovery period. This is commonly called risk tolerance. When evaluating the type of portfolio to build, financial planners will often get investors to answer questions that help frame the level of risk the investor can tolerate. The ability to ride out the downturns is thought to be essential to the process of avoiding a permanent loss. Of course, this assumes that the markets will recover and generally rise over time at a rate greater than inflation, a fact that is becoming less apparent since the year 2000.

Understanding this relationship between risk and return creates an opportunity to construct portfolios that have many elements to meet many different purposes. Hedge funds that dial in this level of risk to return ratio to improve returns at various levels of risk give investors an advantage over traditional investment solutions. The future of hedge funds becomes something completely different than a simple measure against the US stock market. It becomes a measure of risk and return that aligns the best outcome for the level of risk the investor wishes to take. When measured on this scale, the hedge fund can show a substantial benefit to investors. Even with this understanding, there will be those that measure investment success on the basis of returns alone. Despite being a longshot, high returns will prove to be just too attractive for some investors. This "bet" on Wall Street turns prudent investors into gamblers. Some will get lucky, but most will be on the losing side of the bet.

As previously stated, the structural and behavioral inefficiencies of markets and investors will continue to exist, even in an automated market. The level of these imperfections may decrease over time and the difficulty in identifying them may continue to give hedge fund managers challenges; however, these types of hedge funds can show sustained outperformance until the cause for the imperfection is eliminated. Knowing the cause is the key. Too many hedge fund managers measure the correlation while not understanding the cause. These quantitative measures provide statistical improvement in the hedge fund manager's performance in the short run, but lack sustainability in all market conditions. Once understood, these imperfections can get arbitraged away. That is to say, the conditions that led to the outperformance is soon known by all and eliminated as a meaningful advantage.

The only exceptions that lead to sustained outperformance from structural and behavioral inefficiencies are the secret methods and the small-scale opportunities. Secret methods are best represented by Jim Simons and his "black box" technology. Small-scale opportunities are best represented by Jeff Russo and his low-volatility event/index arbitrage investing. With Simons, the secrets are highly guarded. With Russo, the amount of return potential is limited to a small opportunity set (fund capacity of about $1 billion) that falls well-below the institutional investor's expected fund size of several billion dollars.

Even if they don't have an edge, hedge fund managers can serve a purpose in a non-correlated portfolio. If the hedge fund strategy doesn't show any additional return benefit over other investments of equivalent risk levels, it may be more non-correlated to stocks and bonds than other investments. Additionally, some hedged strategies create upper and lower boundaries for price variation that help determine rebalancing points. Stocks and bonds have shown very wide variation with highly unpredictable limits. Knowing the limits allows for portfolio construction that better models the expected risk each element adds to the portfolio.

Chapter 8 – The Allure of Private Equity

"Success is not final, failure is not fatal: it is the courage to continue that counts."
Winston Churchill

I was 26 years old, and I had just opened my first CPA practice in a small historic mining town in California. I had chosen this area to raise my children primarily because of its rural setting, affordability, and proximity to outdoor recreation. I built a nice CPA practice, but I wanted to do more than just compile financial statements, prepare tax returns, and answer IRS notices. The CPA practice was just a way to pay the bills while I started a real estate development company. I was setting in motion the way that I wanted to build wealth for my family. This was my dream, and it was happening just as I had hoped.

Many dream of building their own business; and, like me, this dream can become a lifelong path of learning and development that leads to destinations never anticipated. While owning your own home is the American dream, owning your own business is at the heart of American freedom. Democracy depends on the independent business person voting with the assurance that neither employer nor government can influence their vote. Thomas Jefferson said about the self-employed farmers of his time, "they are the most vigorous, the most independent, the most virtuous, and they are tied to their country and wedded to its liberty and interests by the most lasting bands." In today's modern world, the independent business person, is the self-employed farmer that Thomas Jefferson so implored us to preserve and grow for the sake of democracy. Private business is the stuff that made America. It is what drove men to leave country, family, and the security of things known to come to the land of opportunity and make something of themselves and for their families. It is what allows our passions to be expressed through our hands, minds, and hearts. Owning your own business is the ultimate expression of being American, and Private Equity is the source of capital that helps make that a reality.

Starting in the early 1970s, US factories began to close and good-paying employment opportunities left the American mega-companies. Some expansion into new industries continued outpacing contraction until the peak of manufacturing employment in June 1979. For those able, retraining and education led to employment in the fastest growing industry, technology.

I landed in Silicon Valley, the heart of the technology boom, in June of 1981. Names like Microsoft and Apple where just starting to be known. One of my first jobs as a Price Waterhouse employee was to figure out how to use the Apple II computer. A personal computer was something never seen before by many of my colleagues. I was selected for the job because I had the most programming experience having been an engineering student at one time. If you had any science or math training, jobs in technology were easy to find.

My generation of college graduates had technology as an option for our careers. Rather than becoming an accountant or manager in a manufacturing company, we could ride the growth wave of the technology boom. While our fathers and older brothers were getting laid off from their manufacturing jobs, we had good entry-level positions available in technology. At first, these jobs were mostly with large firms like Hewlett Packard and IBM, but soon smaller tech start-ups would become the new gold rush for small business entrepreneurs.

The shift from manufacturing to tech was faster than most had anticipated. Fortunately, someone had to build the cabinets to house the electronics, and chip technology was manufacturing based. This gave former assembly line workers a job option if they were willing to relocate. By the late 1990s, even these jobs were starting to be "outsourced" to places like China, India, and Mexico. Between June of 1979 and June 1999, manufacturing jobs dropped from 19.6 million to 17.3 million; however, by June of 2015, manufacturing jobs dropped to just 12.3 million. It took 20 years to lose 11.3% of the peak level jobs in manufacturing and only 16 more years to lose another 25.9% (these and the following labor statistics are from the US Bureau of Labor Statistics). Again, the year 2000 was the inflection point when good-paying jobs for the average American began to drop off rapidly. During that same 36 year period, the labor force rose by over 50%. The effective impact of having a significantly smaller percentage of the jobs come from manufacturing was felt in the average American household as a lower living standard.

Manufacturing wasn't the only industry to lose employment. Natural resources lost jobs as well. Farmers and miners found it hard to stay small or compete with the overseas low-cost labor markets. The shift from traditional labor opportunities to more technical positions had begun. This was especially true in the Financial Service industry where total jobs went up almost 68% in the same 36 year period. Surprisingly, the Information industry didn't expand much during this period, growing only by about 17%; however, the Information industry did peak in 2000 with a growth of about 54% in 21 years. Since the tech bubble burst in 2000, there has been a massive outsourcing of American technology jobs to other countries explaining the rapid decline in jobs in the Information industry.

Americans have shown great resilience to the many economic challenges thrown their way. While small business jobs were hurt significantly more by the financial crisis, small business is making a comeback. The Small Business Administration tracks jobs created by small businesses (defined as less than 500 employees) vs. larger business (500 or more employees). According to the SBA's report on January 15, 2015, "More than 7 million of the 11 million jobs created during our recovery have been generated by startups and small enterprises." This trend has continued into 2015, as well.

Investors have three main ways to participate with these wealth-builders as follows:

1. Co-investment
2. Private Fund
3. Public Stock

Each of the three investment opportunities has advantages, but each poses certain risks, as well. Selecting the right private equity investment can be very profitable for investors, but be warned, there are many failures of private companies. Knowing how to evaluate, buy, support, and sell private equity investments takes skill and experience that are often best left to the professionals.

Co-investing is the most direct way to participate in the building of a private company. If you can't or don't want to run the business yourself, using some of your investment capital to support another skilled business professional may be appealing to you. This type of investing comes with several risks. First, the ability to get your money back may be limited for several years. Second, it is difficult to value a private company. Even with appraisals, the value agreed upon is just an estimate based on many unknown future outcomes. Another risk is that of future capital needs. Some private companies have several rounds of capital raises. This may mean you are called upon to put more funds into the company. If you don't participate in future rounds of capital raises, your position could get diluted, reducing the returns you would expect from the investment.

Private Fund investing, also called a Private Equity Fund, is one of the most common ways to invest in private businesses. A professional manager of the fund does the evaluation of the businesses, negotiates to purchase some or all of the private business equity, and manages the company to effect a rapid growth in its value. This type of investing is generally only available to investors that have a large amount of liquid assets and have had high incomes for the past 2-3 years. Getting out of a private fund investment before the liquidation date (generally in 5-10 years) often means selling it at a discount, if a buyer can even be found. Endowments have been quite aggressively buying these types of investments to enhance total return of their portfolios. It is thought that there is an "illiquidity premium" with private equity. This is the added return for locking up your investment for several years. Additionally, endowment managers see private equity as having some non-correlation with public stocks. This helps reduce the overall risk of the endowment.

Investing in the public stock of companies that buy private firms is another indirect way to participate in the benefits of private companies. There are several public companies that do this either exclusively or as part of an overall investment strategy. The benefits of this form of investing is the daily liquidity of a public stock. While the return expectations are generally lower than a co-investment or private fund investment, the opportunity to rebalance or quickly exit your investment may be quite appealing to certain investors.

Private equity investing isn't new. In the 1980's limited partnership investments (i.e., private equity) became quite popular. The movie "The Boost" with James Wood showed how money from these investment sales fueled the drug-filled lives of many financial professionals. Unfortunately, many of these investments failed and cost the investors all of their investment and more in some cases. Most of these limited partnerships were tax-based schemes that had little business merit. When the 1986 tax act became fully implemented in 1990, most of these schemes went under as the tax benefits dried up.

Venture capital, an early stage investment in a business, became the investment choice of private equity in the 1990s. This fueled the dot com era of investing that eventually resulted in the tech bubble bursting in 2000. Venture capital continues in various forms today including the most recent form of Crowdfunding. Like most fads, many poorly-designed business plans get funded and ultimately fail, but there are many rags to riches stories in the venture capital world. Its "get rich quick" format attracts those who are willing to take a high-risk bet.

The most successful venture investors are those who can mentor the emerging company through the growth phases until the company has stabilized and can exist on its own operations. These venture capitalists know how to set up the various pieces needed to get the company to a positive cash flow with good growth expectations. What's more, the venture capitalist knows how to do this quickly and sell their own equity in the venture at the point of peak returns.

Leveraged buyouts is another form of private equity investing. This was popular in the 2000s following the tech bubble bursting. The idea is to acquire a company with very little initial investment and a lot of debt. The trick is to make sure the company's cash flow can support the debt. This works well when interest rates on debt are substantially lower than the expected returns of the equity investors. If a company can be valued with a 15% return on investment expectation but bought with an 8% debt obligation, the spread between 8% and 15% creates value. This is a bit complicated, but the math models for these deals made billions for the investment bankers and private equity investors who had access to low-cost debt.

In the non-correlated investment strategies described in this book, private equity investments that lock up the investment for several years create a limitation on the variation alpha that can be created from the natural volatility of the investment. The Public Stock version does give additional opportunity to generate variation alpha, but the return given up to get liquidity sometimes doesn't offset the variation alpha that can be generated.

Considering these qualities, the private equity investment tends to be a difficult choice in a non-correlated portfolio that seeks to generate variation alpha. That doesn't mean that investors should not consider private equity as a possible supplement to their wealth-building efforts. Finding a good co-investment like a real estate rehab project with a trusted contractor, or a tech venture with an experienced engineer could prove to be a good source of additional wealth. Be cautious in your choices, as the risky nature of these investments can result in a total loss. In a prudent financial plan, the private equity investment would come after your own wealth-building efforts are funded, a significant amount of liquid savings has been accumulated, and you have a good base of investments to support your future goals.

One new form of private equity investing was made possible with the Jobs Act ('Jumpstart Our Business Startups Act," April 5, 2012). In this Act, a new form of investing was made possible called Crowdfunding. Meant to allow internet technology to establish a platform for matching businesses in need of capital with investors. It uniquely allows for many small investments (i.e., a crowd) to fund the business. This spreads the risk over a wider population and gives the average investor the chance to participate in the wealth-building activities of companies they want to support.

In principle, the idea of crowdfunding has merit. The details of how this gets done is much more complex. Many of the pioneers of this emerging business model believe crowdfunding will fill the gap left in middle-market investment banking (the $10-$500 million space). The smaller tech projects seem to be getting the bulk of the flows. According to a Forbes article published June 9, 2015, "By 2016 the crowdfunding industry is on track to account for more funding than venture capital, according to a recent report by Massolution." The author of this article, Chance Barnett, goes on to write, "Fast forward to today and we saw $16 billion crowdfunded in 2014, with 2015 estimated to grow to over $34 billion. In comparison, the VC industry invests an average of $30 billion each year." This is an investment option to watch, but expect some typical new product speed bumps along the way. We have yet to see the first major fraud come out of crowdfunding, but regulators and state attorney generals are moving rapidly to tighten up the consumer protections.

In summary, private equity is a hybrid of wealth building and investing. It provides a passive solution to participate in the wealth-building efforts of others. Many private equity offerings put limits on liquidity. This creates limits on the ability to generate variation alpha if included in an investment portfolio. As such, it is easier to consider private equity as a third category of asset allocation to follow after wealth building and investment portfolios are at levels needed to meet financial goals. Relying on private equity to be a substitute for wealth building or as a long-term solution for an investment portfolio may insert too much risk into a financial plan. Consider proceeding slowly into this world, and consider using public stock of private equity firms as the early-stage form for this category of asset allocation.

Chapter 9 – Bad Science and False Beliefs

"The greatest deception men suffer is from their own opinions."

Leonardo da Vinci

While speaking with a chief investment officer (CIO) for a good-sized investment firm, I mentioned Malkiels work on measuring the effectiveness of picking stocks and calling markets. With some surprise on my part, the CIO said that he did not subscribe to the work at Princeton University, implying that he thought he could be predictive with his investment approach. Generally, I would have expected someone of that level to acknowledge the many studies confirming the work first published out of Princeton University, but the CIO truly believed he could predict the financial future. Rather than embarrass the CIO with a request for confirmation of his statement, I moved passed his prophetic claims. I then ask about his desire to rebalance away from an investment that had recently trended down but would protect his portfolios in a market downturn. He stated that he only wanted investments that went up. Even though global stock markets took a major correction right after this conversation, it is unlikely that the CIO learned anything from his clients' investment losses. Often these two beliefs go hand-in-hand – 1) I can predict the future or react quickly enough to sell out of declining markets and 2) I should only keep investments that have gone up and sell the ones that disappoint me and go down. This CIO was selling hope to his clients. He really didn't have a sustainable strategy, only the belief that markets always go up over time and that he can find the part of the markets that goes up the fastest.

This CIO had become subject to a common behavior called Confirmation Bias. His results were viewed as confirming his belief system rather than actually being measured for statistical accuracy. This reminded me of the story of 100 investment managers around a table. With each flip of a coin, fewer and fewer advisers had guessed the outcome of the coin flip, correctly. The last adviser to guess right was declared the guru of investing. This process of sequential success in guessing stock market outcomes ultimately results in a statistical reversion to the market, and in most studies, to a result that is less than market returns. Unfortunately, human behavior tends to look for confirmation of any belief we hold and reinforce that belief in the outcomes we observe. Whether in our faith or in our careers, we form a mental map of our world and project that onto the world around us. It is very difficult for us to repaint our mental maps and adopt new beliefs.

When it comes to a non-correlated approach to investing, it takes complete acknowledgement that the events of the world are subject to many forces that we currently have difficulty knowing or measuring. These forces can be sudden and unexpected, even though after the fact we may feel we should have seen it coming. Our overestimate of the foreseeability of outcomes after the event is called hindsight bias. We muse, "We should have seen the tech bubble coming in 1999. After all, companies shouldn't get those types of valuations without a correction." Confirming our hindsight bias, we assert, "The financial crisis certainly was predictable, too. John Paulson and Nouriel Roubini knew it was coming and tried to warn us. Next time, we will know better." If we are to acknowledge this bias and open our minds to the possibility that predicting the financial markets has no long-term benefit, we must first recognize the bias we have in evaluating outcomes. Once we say, "I could be wrong," we take the first step in doing the math to find out the actual experience we have with predicting the markets.

Knowing that we can be right many times in a row, doesn't mean that we won't be terribly wrong at some point in the future. The history of the markets is for sudden and precipitous drops that take most investors by surprise. The October 19, 1987 drop of over 20% stands as the greatest single day drop in the S&P 500 index. The September 19, 2008 S&P 500 close was 1255.07. By October 10, 2008, the S&P 500 closed at 899.22, a 28% decline.

"Just hang in there. It will come back." This is the only comfort the predictive investment manager can offer. It is in these big corrections that the investment manager finds that their apparent genius has been in fact a simple participation in the ebb and flow of market tides. This "tail risk," as it is known, becomes a disaster for the investing public and brings humility to the once "smart" investment manager. For those betting against the tide, they become the new geniuses of the market. When averaged out, the majority of the players in the prediction game have returns very similar to the market. For those that gamble and guess the correct outcome, they become our new gurus of investing, at least until they disappoint us.

Outcome bias is when a decision is judged in light of a later outcome, even though the outcome may have been from other factors. To illustrate this, let's look at the false sense of security that the post financial crisis volatility has created. There have been many small "dips" in the stock market since March of 2009. Some have been as big as 20% dips as in August 2011. How does the investment manager know if it is a dip, or a crash? If the stock market goes down 5% today, is that a dip or the start of a 45% decline that will not be recovered for 5+ years? What if the dip goes to -10% the next day? -15% the third? Each day the investment adviser has to gamble on their predictions. The previous outcomes have little to do with the next outcome. It is somewhat like a blackjack player believing they will win the next hand just because they have lost several in a row. The many dips that have occurred creates a false sense of predictability. The investment manager begins to think that they can predict the outcome because each time there was a dip, the market came back and rewarded them for staying invested or buying the dip.

I heard many investment advisers saying they knew that the Lehman investment bank failure in Sept 2008 created a very predictable outcome, but very few had the authority, liquidity, or real knowledge to step out of the way of the ensuing tsunamis of financial losses. Even if they did know, where would they put the cash from liquidating their stocks? Both bonds and some cash instruments went down in the financial crisis. The actual measure of their behavior proves differently than the Outcome Bias they hold. That is not to say that some investment managers didn't actually succeed over time. It is this phenomena that we will examine next.

We love hearing stories more than being given statistical analysis. This is one investor bias that is well known. This book is a story to explain certain analysis that I have conducted in measuring and evaluating the effectiveness of our industry in constructing predictive portfolios in contrast to using a non-correlated endowment method to investing. Storytelling by its nature is entertaining, but it can be used to mask the truth about the analysis. This bias to storytelling gives the effective storyteller the advantage over the analyst. The age of the internet has exposed many investment industry falsehoods wrapped in a good story, including those falsehoods about certain managers who truly have an edge in their investment predictions. While many may claim an edge, analysis sometimes proves otherwise.

The internet community loves to expose those claiming better crystal balls (or black boxes) to analysis of the facts. Investment gurus are no exception. A simple examination of these gurus reveals some interesting information about our own need for heroes. In an attempt to order the world, investors want to believe "father/mother knows best" applies to these investment professionals. They tell a compelling story. They have correlation charts to prove their point. Nevertheless, a simple search of the internet generally exposes the factor bet or other reporting trick that the Guru is doing to "outperform" the market.

Jim Rogers is one of those gurus of investing that has one of the best track records in the history of fund management. He co-founded the Quantum fund that more than significantly outperformed the US stock market in its first 10 years. After just seven years (1973-1980), Rogers retired at the young age of 37 to enjoy the life of an adventurer, author, professor, and media commentator.

Now, a well followed proponent of commodities investing and a resident of China, Rogers is putting on his forecasting hat to call another market run. In May 2015, Rogers commented on the nearly 5,000 level reached by the Shanghai stock market predicting that it would go to 6,000. He did qualify his comments saying that he hoped this market would pullback somewhat to avoid a bubble.

While the returns that Rogers and his business partner, George

Soros, created in the 1970s were nothing short of amazing, the best forecasters, can make predictions that give investors the wrong impression. Rogers did not say when the 6,000 mark would be reached on the Shanghai market, and he did not say how much the pullback would be. The impression many had after this statement was that the Shanghai stock market would continue to rise another 20% after already more than doubling the prior year. Investors who took that bet would be surprised to see the Shanghai market drop to under 3,000 before the end of August. Jim Rogers may be right, but it may take some time before the 6,000 mark will be seen. The "somewhat" pullback he wanted to avoid a bubble was a drop of over 40% from the market highs.

Predicting, no matter how mathematical or empirically based, has the element of human behavior as a driving force for stock and bond pricing. Jim Rogers could not see the short-term impacts of the Chinese economic slowdown or effects of the devaluation of the Chinese currency. If he had, he may have warned investors to wait before jumping into the market.

Guru status did not guarantee Rogers that all his predictions would be accurate on both the amount and the timing. Just because Rogers was right before did not guarantee he would be right again. That's because the best predictions always have the unexpected event that can materially alter the prediction. These events come in many forms but result in, often unpredictable, reactions by investors that drive the pricing of securities markets. Even if the predictions include the possibility of the event, the human behavior in reaction to the event is even more difficult to predict.

Rogers, Soros, and other great investors often have an edge on knowing how a fairly short-term event will impact a commodity, company, or market. This edge gives them the advantage they need to outperform. It is somewhat like knowing that the roulette wheel favors a particular quadrant or playing cards with a marked deck. This edge is hard to protect and often has limits on its size. Other investors soon learn of the edge and begin to use it, too. This can spread the limited benefit of this knowledge over more investors. Soon, the regulators identify the impact of this trade and make changes to the trading rules to try and eliminate this knowledge favoring any one investor or group of investors.

As market information becomes more and more efficient (the internet providing a big leap forward in this regard), the techniques to prove your superior abilities change, too. This often leads to "real advantage" giving way to "perceived advantage." The illusion of an investing edge can be just as profitable as the actual edge. There are many ways that these modern-day gurus are creating the illusion. Even very sophisticated investors can fall for some of these tricks.

I like to categorize the three basic investment snake oil pitches as follows:

- Index Tricks – Using the wrong index to make performance look better
- Time Travel – Picking a time period to show successes and mask failures
- Herding – Announcing intentions to get followers to create self-fulfilling prophecy.

With Index Tricks, the investment manager compares performance to an index that has little to do with the actual strategy. It is natural for investors to want to compare performance to something that will benchmark the strategy. This gives the investor something to judge the skill of the investment professional. Forgetting what has been learned so far about calling markets and picking stocks as having little benefit, the typical investor looks for someone who has a strategy that is working better than some other strategy.

The investment managers knows that beating a benchmark, generally a published index, will have a positive effect on getting more assets under management. Most investment managers cannot beat their benchmarks by any measurable level unless they take a gamble and get lucky. Most managers prefer not to take gambles. Instead, they tend choose benchmarks that make them look better.

One of the first places I learned about index tricks was a U.S. large-cap core fund from a well-known asset manager. One year, the fund's portfolio manager outperformed by about 9% over the benchmark. Outperforming by 1% in a year would be considered exceptional for such a strategy. The reason was quite simple. He added small-cap stocks to his portfolio during a time that small cap was outperforming. His fund should have been reclassified and compared to another index, but it wasn't. You could say that was a smart move to add small-cap stocks. I'm sure most investors wouldn't mind that outperformance. Small cap stocks tends to be more volatile and had a bad year the next year. He gave back all of that outperformance as a result.

One of the ways to spot an index trick is to measure the correlation between the index and the strategy. If it is low, this could mean that the wrong index is being used. Alternative strategies often want to be non-correlated, and an inappropriate index will sometimes be intentionally chosen to make the non-correlation look even better.

Sometimes it is hard to find an index that actually fits the strategy. For example, a multi-cap fund may have an intentional bias towards large, mid, or small cap. If that bias places the fund outside the average of multi-cap funds, a multi-cap benchmark may not be a good measure for that fund. Making a benchmark or custom index to measure the strategy may be the best way to approach a performance evaluation. This is especially true of global allocation funds. These funds hold both stocks and bonds. One of the most popular global allocation funds advertises that it beat a global stock index every rolling 10-year period. The reason wasn't the stocks, but the bonds it held. With bonds in a 30-year bull market and stocks always crashing sometime during a 10-year rolling period, the global allocation fund looked rather appealing next to a stock index.

Time Travel deceptions are very common. This is where presentations show valley-to-peak performance periods or exceptionally long periods to mask big variations in performance. Running performance for different time periods helps highlight what's missing from the valley-to-peak presentations. Looking at volatility and beta often highlight the reasons for long-cycle deceptions. Another technique is the use of a dispersion chart (showing a count of good and bad performance) and max-drawdown numbers to see if there are any big "tail" risks.

Herding is probably the most difficult to measure and discover. This is the process of getting other investor behavior to drive up or down stocks. This takes a following to accomplish. One example is for a "Guru" to talk up a stock, market, or industry after they purchased a big position in it. You will hear "he puts his money where his mouth is" as a justification for this behavior. The reality is that Guru just wants the "lift" from his followers buying up the position(s) after he does. During volatile periods in markets, the Guru may switch his tune and talk down the stock, market, or industry. Check the level of short positions the Guru has and you will find he will profit from the "drag" his followers give a stock(s) when they sell out.

One of the most common herding effects come from TV investment stars. Entertaining as they might be, the actual performance of these wizards of the air waves is hard to measure. Notice they may tell you if they like or dislike a stock or segment of the market, but they never give you dates and times to trade into and out of the positions or the percentage allocation that you should include in your portfolio.

One of the behaviors of Wall Street that many found distasteful was the use of research opinions to drive up/down stocks that benefited the proprietary holdings or relationships of the research firm. One famous research analyst was barred from the industry after giving a top rating to a stock while privately emailing to members of his firm that it was a bad investment. Shortly after this incident became public, new regulations helped clean up this behavior.

Even with these new regulations, some broker dealers still use research to influence a move in securities used in some of their publicly marketed portfolios. They will look at what securities are held in the separate accounts and funds managed by their firm and find ways to justify the research opinions that help those positions.

Doesn't it seem odd that long-only equity portfolio managers always seem to be optimistic about stocks going up and bond managers always point to the safety of bond investments? We know that not to be true, but we want to follow the advice of these famous investment professionals. Just because an investment professional is on television or publishes a popular newsletter doesn't mean they can predict the direction of stock of bond investments. Knowing how to spot their techniques they use to convince you of their ability gives you knowledge to use in making wise decisions with your investment portfolios.

Chapter 10 – Don't Invest In Me

"An investment in knowledge pays the best interest."

Benjamin Franklin

This chapter is written with some ideas that may seem difficult for new investors. Rather than explain every concept in this chapter, I chose to let the readers use this as a self-assessment tool. If the ideas make sense, you may be ready to move forward with implementation of a non-correlated investment strategy. Don't let the complexity discourage you. If it is too confusing, find a good adviser who knows how to manage this way and hire that adviser to help you. Even if you do understand the concepts, you may still want to seek help if you don't have the time or inclination to do this yourself.

For those investors who want to manage their own accounts, this chapter is for you. It gives you the steps I found that work in the current climate for investing. Understand that things can change. This approach to investing may become less attractive as economies and investment opportunities change. I developed this approach because I saw that the old approach of "buying the market" had stopped giving investors an adequate return for the risk they were taking.

If you can manage and trade your own investments, if you can educate yourself on how to construct a non-correlated portfolio, if you can afford the tools and systems to monitor and evaluate the performance and risk of your portfolio, doing it yourself is the best way to invest. While many financial advisers will say that they put your interests before their own, few will have the same concern for your financial success as you do. Manage your own investments, if you can. It is the best way to assure successful achievement of your financial goals. So, why would anyone hire an investment adviser?

I often ask my clients, "Do you have the time, the money, and the education to manage your investments?" My firm is set up to efficiently manage for many clients. This reduces the amount of time that we spend on each dollar invested as compared to you managing just your own account; we monitor our clients' accounts with expensive systems that perform complex mathematical analysis to evaluate the way each investment is reacting to the market and economic forces; and we hire and train staff that have focused their education on disciplines that benefit our methods of investing. Even though I may have an advantage over what my clients are able to do, I still say "Don't invest _in_ me."

This may sound a bit strange given that I earn a living by managing my clients' investments. The key word here is "in." Too often, investors become followers of a guru of investing and completely stop thinking for themselves. This is a dangerous practice. These type of investors invest "in" the investment manager and forget why they selected the manager in the first place. My advice is to invest "with" the investment adviser that best fits your approach to investing. Investing "with" an adviser means that you control the instructions that go with your account; you keep the adviser aligned with your self-interests; and you keep your investments with a separate custodian to avoid having the investment adviser misappropriate your funds.

My best advocate is an educated client. When my clients understand why I managed the way that I do, they become great spokespeople for my firm. I welcome questions from my clients. I like it when I hear questions like "Why were you in cash during the last rebalance?" or "Why did you sell out of that investment?" This is a chance for my clients to become better educated on the management of their money. It also gives me feedback to better align their investment strategy to their goals. As clients invest in their education, they become better able to express their ideas about investing and have better outcomes to meet their goals.

With that said, the remainder of this book will be on the mechanics of building a non-correlated portfolio using principles employed in the Endowment Method with enhancements I discovered from added liquidity. The first step in any strategy is to state the assumptions. The first assumption of this strategy is that predicting market or stock direction does not help improve returns. While predictions may be effective in the short run, sudden and unexpected changes in the directional movement of the market or stock trend can remove any gains made through previous predictive success. This does not imply that quantitative methods and fundamental research are without value. Avoiding a bad decision can still be an effective part of a reactive strategy. The benefit of research primarily becomes avoiding the areas where pitfalls are likely to occur. It is akin to walking through a mine field. If you see the mine, don't step on it. Don't just assume all mines are hidden. So too with security market changes. If you see something like the Lehman Brothers failure of 2008, it certainly sends a signal about how investors will react and what to avoid in your investment selections.

Therefore, the second assumption of this strategy is that tilting the portfolio away from potential trouble is better than a fixed allocation approach. This is one of the assumptions where I feel more research is needed. This is based more on experience than empirical evidence. Unlike most asset allocators who look for outperformance, we look to avoid underperformance. In baseball language, it is easier to predict a strikeout than a home run. The nature of a reactive approach does not mean that downturns have no effect on pricing of securities. It just means that opportunities for variation alpha are created. Total return of a portfolio still includes the performance of the underlying securities. Avoiding poor performing securities will still have a positive impact on the total portfolio performance. Essentially, this second assumption views predicting bad performance as more successful than predicting good performance.

The third assumption of this strategy is that fixed income investments have become more correlated to equity investments, especially during times of market or economic stress, and provide less protection than certain alternative investments that have shown more consistent non-correlation to equity markets. Certainly, there are examples of alternative investments that have higher correlations with equity markets or that trend to higher correlation under certain market or economic conditions; however, this third assumption of the strategy is focused on finding alternative investments that remain highly non-correlated. With current conditions, fixed income investments have become less attractive than say 30 years ago when rates were peaking at all-time highs. With low rates and the negative impact on valuations from of rising rates, fixed income investments have become less attractive than in previous years. Additionally, fixed income investments have had increased correlations in times of stress thereby increasing portfolio losses instead of counterbalancing declines in equity markets.

The fourth assumption of this strategy is that the range of variation in some non-correlated investments tends to have more predictable limits than do the equity and bond markets. This does not mean that the direction of the variation is predictable, but that the limits of the variation tend to be more defined. The equity markets showed a six sigma variation in the 2000-2002 tech bubble burst and a seven sigma variation in the 2007-2009 financial crisis. Many are looking for an eight sigma down turn with the next market crisis. These ever increasing ranges of variation create increasing risk that can be opportunities for increased alpha generation in a non-correlated portfolio.

The opposite can be said for a predictive portfolio strategy in that the increase in equity market variation creates an increased chance of failure. While the opportunity for variation alpha is greater, the ability to extract that potential decreases when the limits of the variation are constantly changing. Variation alpha is maximized when rebalancing occurs at the peaks and valleys of the variation. Many types of alternative investments seek to limit these ranges of variation placing caps and floors on the peaks and valleys. The more predictable the range, the more variation alpha produced.

The fifth assumption of this strategy is that market liquidity will be adequate to support the rebalancing of portfolios that employ a non-correlated strategy. Experience has taught me that this strategy tends to be buying what others are selling and selling what others are buying during a rebalance. As equity and bond markets decline, predictive (traditional) strategies are rebalancing to step out of the way of the downturn. Generally, it takes time to sell out of these declining positions. By the time buyers show up, the predictive strategy has already lost a good portion of value in the positions it is selling. Conversely, a non-correlated portfolio is buying up the undervalued positions with funds generated from sale of its performing components. Predictive strategies move from their declining positions to positions that are showing strength. The positions that are strengthening are the very positions that non-correlated strategies are selling to raise cash to buy up the declining positions. This naturally creates a liquidity source for non-correlated portfolios during periods when liquidity is needed.

The sixth assumption is that the movement of the non-correlation groups will occur with enough frequency and/or size of movement to generate potential variation alpha that can be extracted with a rebalance of the portfolio. Extracting performance from the movement of the portfolio elements requires that the move be with enough energy (frequency x amplitude) to make it worthwhile to rebalance. Rebalances have costs and timing risks that need to be sufficiently low enough to allow for the rebalance benefits to create a net increase in overall portfolio performance. The studies I conducted showed that having several non-correlated groups within the portfolio aided in reducing overall portfolio risk while giving the opportunity to increase frequency and/or amplitude of each investible element. Essentially, the portfolio's overall risk could be controlled with the non-correlation while allowing for the risk of the individual elements to rise to much higher levels than would normally be acceptable for the client's risk tolerance.

The last assumption is that the non-correlated investments used in the portfolio do not suffer from diminished return-to-risk ratios. This is important in considering a non-correlated portfolio. Over long cycles of investing, the return-to-risk ratio influences overall performance for the risk levels targeted. The benefits derived from the non-correlation should not be offset by a diminished return experience from achieving non-correlation. Fortunately, good risk-managed, long-short funds tend to show higher return-to-risk ratios than traditional long-only investments. As such, we find that the non-correlated alternative investment strategies we select actually improve returns from both non-correlation relative to other investments in the portfolio (variation alpha) and from improved risk-to-return ratios the alternative investment manager achieves through effective investment strategies (manager alpha).

The construction of a non-correlated portfolio requires careful evaluation of the potential risks that exist in the securities markets and the economies influencing those securities markets. The asset allocation model (the model) used in the construction of this type of portfolio should reflect thoughtful avoidance of pitfalls. This requires a model that considers certain key data to steer the portfolio around the higher risk items. Leading indicators of potential risk need to be considered when employing a strategy like this. These indicators are merely flashing lights warning investors of upcoming dangers that should be considered. In my experience, additional return can be achieved through minor tactical moves in the allocation percentages. The precision of these moves is still evolving. Like most good strategies, the adaptive nature of this model will allow for improvement over time.

My approach is to break the allocation into two parts – Beta and Alpha. The Beta components are those normally found in predictive strategies. The Alpha components are generally composed of a variety of investments that are not expected to correlate to the Beta elements or to each other. The ratio between the Beta and the Alpha components depends on certain indicators of economic health, market movement, and risk. Historically, the optimized ratio is around 50% to Beta and 50% to Alpha. The model seeks to avoid a Beta downturn (like 2007-2009) through a tilt of its allocation to Alpha during higher risk periods. Conversely, the model seeks to avoid an underperformance period from Alpha managers (like 2009-2015) by tilting the portfolio towards Beta.

Within the Beta components, my model breaks down the allocation to Equity and Fixed Income. The Fixed Income allocation percentage is determined by an algorithm that looks at several indicators of credit risk, economic health, and recent interest rate history. This analysis seeks to reduce fixed income allocations during times of underperformance. The model uses substantially less fixed income than other similar risk-adjusted allocation models because of two factors. First, fixed income plays less of a risk-reducing role in non-correlated portfolios due to the protective nature of the type of non-correlated alternative investments used in the model. Second, the reduced amplitude and frequency of variation in many fixed income securities makes them less attractive for generation of variation alpha.

For the Equity allocation in the Beta components, I employ a technical model that ranks 13 elements based on various factors. While predictive in nature, the degree of tilt is limited to a minor amount of variation. The goal of this breakdown of the equity elements is to provide opportunities for variation alpha during normal swings in performance. To reduce single stock risk and trading costs (free trades in most cases), I use ETFs. The elements we use are eight sector ETFs, three market-cap ETFs (large/mid/small), and two international (developed and emerging) ETFs. While there may be some additional granularity available (like cap size in the international allocations), I haven't found significant benefit from adding it to my clients' portfolios.

Within the Alpha components, the model has two categories – 1) Non-correlated and 2) Thematic. The Non-correlated portion is allocated to investments that are thought to have consistently low correlation to the Beta portion of the portfolio and to each other. The Thematic portion has non-correlation due to certain current conditions in the markets or economy, which are expected to change over time. These Thematic investments can have periods of correlation with Beta or other Alpha components but are experiencing positive current results that are non-correlated to the other elements of the portfolio. As such, the allocation to an individual thematic element is thought to be temporary and could be removed as correlations increase.

The model provides for three levels of investor risk tolerance by adjusting allocations to securities with differing risk profiles. The "Optimized" version utilizes allocation percentages that seek to maximize the return for a moderate level of volatility. The "Conservative" portfolio reduces exposures to higher risk elements and increases exposures to lower risk elements in an effort to provide greater capital preservation. The "Return Focused" allocates more to elements thought to have higher individual volatility; however, Return Focused allocations may not actually result in higher portfolio volatility especially if the non-correlation aspects mute overall portfolio risk. Return Focused portfolios seek higher returns over longer investment cycles.

To implement a similar approach with your own investment portfolio, you would need to identify the allocation approach most appropriate to your investment assumptions and aligned with your investment goals. The approach I take in tilting the portfolio away from potential pitfalls is complex and requires a significant amount of research and data. As such, you may want to design a simpler version for your allocation model. To do this, focus on the non-correlation of each element first. This will allow you to build a portfolio with a higher probability of risk control. Second, select investments that have the highest level of volatility you can tolerate in order to maximize the variation alpha opportunities. Finally, make sure that you incorporate a monitoring and rebalancing process that extracts the energy of the non-correlated movement within your portfolio. If you find that this paragraph is hard to understand, you may want to hire an adviser to assist you while you develop your investment skills.

Now that I have described the portfolio construction steps, you should have the basic tools to build a non-correlated portfolio on your own. Even though the methods I use for my clients for constructing and maintaining their portfolios are somewhat proprietary and involve complex systems, the majority of benefit derived from this approach can be achieved by the average investor with tools readily available from most discount broker dealer custodians (i.e., Fidelity, TD Ameritrade, Schwab…). Several considerations need to be made before embarking on this effort including the selection of a custodian, trading costs of the investments selected, methods and tools for monitoring and rebalancing, and the time it takes to execute an effective strategy. In short, you need three things to be effective in this effort – knowledge, time, and commitment. If one of these three elements are missing, consider hiring an investment adviser to assist you.

The last piece of advice I will give you in constructing this type of portfolio is be patient. When markets are ripping skyward, this approach will likely be underperforming; however, when markets are crashing, you will likely be happy you moved to this approach. Don't get tempted to try and time the markets. Be patient. Just because the market went down 20% doesn't mean it will go back up. Sometimes it continues to go down. Use a systematic approach that removes the emotions from your investment decisions. This will help you keep a patient attitude towards achieving your investment goals.

This is not a method of investing for those that only go with the herd. An entire industry is built around the notion that predicting markets and picking stocks works. Using this method of investing will put you outside the retail investment box.

Additionally, you will be tempted to want to try and outsmart the markets. Just like the gambler that keeps trying to beat the odds, investors keep trying to take the bet their brokers offer. Like the gambler that lets it ride, the investor that stays in the market ultimately has big losses that wipe out all previous winnings. What good is it to win nine times in a row if the tenth time erases all gains? This is the investment game you have been asked to play, but can avoid by using the methods described in this book. Don't bet on Wall Street. Bet on your own ability and good sense.

The results that endowment managers have achieved are just a sample of the success available with this approach. I wish you the best in your efforts to achieve your financial goals. If there is anything I or my firm can do to help you find "Stress-Free Wealth," we would be happy to help. Most of all, I wish for you the wealth of a well-lived life. Just remember…

Don't Take The Bet!